Lecture Notes in Economics and Mathematical Systems

606

Sven von Widekind

Evolution of Non-Expected Utility Preferences

 Springer

Dr. Sven von Widekind
Institute of Mathematical Economics
Bielefeld University
Universitätsstraße 25
33615 Bielefeld
Germany
sven.von_widekind@wiwi.uni-bielefeld.de

ISBN 978-3-540-76841-8   e-ISBN 978-3-540-76845-6

DOI 10.1007/978-3-540-76845-6

Lecture Notes in Economics and Mathematical Systems ISSN 0075-8442

Library of Congress Control Number: 2007941068

© 2008 Springer-Verlag Berlin Heidelberg

Production: LE-TEX Jelonek, Schmidt & Vöckler GbR, Leipzig
Cover design: WMX Design GmbH, Heidelberg

Printed on acid-free paper

9 8 7 6 5 4 3 2 1

springer.com

"It is clear that Economics if it is to be a science at all, must be a mathematical one." (W. St. Jevons, 1871)

Preface

This monograph has been prepared as my doctoral thesis in Economics at the Institute of Mathematical Economics (IMW), Bielefeld University, Germany. The dissertation has been accepted by the Department of Business Administration and Economics (Examiners: Prof. Dr. Walter Trockel and Prof. em. Dr. Joachim Rosenmüller). It has successfully been defended on June 13, 2007.

With this work I strive to complement the recent literature on the evolution of preferences by investigating the non-expected utility case. I have divided the book into seven chapters. An introduction to the topic is given in Chap. 1. In the following Chap. 2 the main model is presented, followed by an analysis of existence issues concerning stable populations. This chapter is preceded by a section reviewing some basic concepts from the theory of choice and game theory. Although I assume that most readers are familiar with these ideas they are recalled primarily in order to assure a common understanding of the terminology. Chap. 3 discusses the results from the previous chapter by means of some examples. A study of the performance of non-expected utility preferences compared to expected utility ones is the subject of Chap. 4. The impact of an important variant of the type space is investigated in Chap. 5. After this, in Chap. 6, I provide an outlook to further possible modifications of the model. Eventually, I summarize and discuss all main findings in Chap. 7.

The preparation of this monograph has greatly benefited from the aid of a number of people. In particular, I wish to express my deepest gratitude to my doctoral advisors Walter Trockel and Joachim Rosenmüller for all their support and encouragement over the past years. Moreover, a lot of valuable comments from Wulf Albers, Alain Chateauneuf, Herbert Dawid, Eddie Dekel, Peter Klibanoff, Jean-

Philippe Lefort and Frank Riedel have contributed substantially to this work. I also like to thank seminar and workshop audiences at the IMW, Bielefeld University and Université Paris 1 Panthéon-Sorbonne as well as at the SAET conference 2007 in Kos, Greece. Special thanks go to my fellow doctoral students and friends Mark Hahmeier, Marten Hillebrand and Olaf Schmitz. Their suggestions helped improving the legibility of the exposition enormously. On the technical site I am much obliged to Matthias Schleef who has helped me overcoming any imaginable difficulties with LaTeX.

Furthermore, I am indebted to the Managerial Economics and Decision Sciences Department (MEDS) at the J. L. Kellogg School of Management at Northwestern University and the Centre d'Economie de la Sorbonne, Université Paris 1 Panthéon-Sorbonne for their hospitality during my visits when parts of this research were conducted. The Ph.D. programs at the Bielefeld Graduate School of Economics and Management (BiGSEM) and the International Research Training Group 'Economic Behavior and Interaction Models' (EBIM) enabled me to receive a comprehensive education in economic theory. Financial support from the German Academic Exchange Service (DAAD), the German Research Foundation (DFG) and the Franco-German University (DFH-UFA) is gratefully acknowledged.

Also, I thank the editors at Springer for their assistance. The collaboration is highly appreciated.

Bielefeld, December 2007   *Sven von Widekind*

Contents

1

Introduction

The theory on the evolution of preferences deals with the endogenous formation of preference relations in strategic situations. It is related to the field of evolutionary game theory. Models are based on the 'indirect evolutionary approach' according to which preferences determine choice behavior which in turn determines evolutionary success. The latter eventually governs the evolution of preferences. Literature usually considers a class of preferences which admit an expected utility representation. In this doctoral monograph we analyze the role and the influence of general, possibly non-expected utility preferences in such an evolutionary setup. In particular, we investigate whether preferences which diverge from von Neumann-Morgenstern expected utility may potentially prove to be successful under evolutionary pressures. Furthermore, we contribute to the research into existence issues for so-called stable populations.

The assumption that an individual decision-maker, or 'agent' for short, possesses a complete and transitive binary relation on a given set of alternatives forms the usual basis of a formal economic modeling of human choice behavior. An agent with such a 'preference relation' is called rational if she always chooses a best one from a given (sub-) set of alternatives in the sense that an available alternative that the individual strictly prefers to the selected one does not exist. Under some continuity assumptions (cf. [12]) the preference relation of a rational agent may be represented by a utility function, i.e. by a real-valued function on the set of alternatives.

In the context of decision-making under risk the final realizations of the alternatives are unknown. Each alternative is now characterized by a set of possible consequences and their respective probabilities of occurrence. It is commonly referred to as a lottery. This approach is different from models on choice under uncertainty where the agent has only a subjective assessment of the probabilities. Early noted contributions to this field are [52] and [3], followed by many others. For an introduction we refer to [30]. The modern theory of choice under risk, however, traces back to John von Neumann and Oskar Morgenstern's expected utility theory ([39]). The so-called independence axiom generates the utility representation of the agent's preference relation on lotteries in the well-known expected utility form while other assumptions on preferences largely amount to assuring existence of a utility function. Von Neumann and Morgenstern's approach has remained the standard model in decision theory under risk. Due to the functional form of the utility representation the expected utility theorem is intuitive and analytically easily applicable to many socio-scientific contexts. As an example which will be at the center of this work, expected utility theory prevails as the decision-theoretic basis of game theory. Other important applications include the theory of finance, e.g. the analysis of optimal investment and portfolio decisions (cf. amongst others [61] and [13]). Despite this popularity, the findings in [2], [27] and [62] reveal expected utility theory's strong limitations as a general descriptive model of individual decision-making under risk. Other important empirical contributions indicating non-rationality of individuals as well as violations of the independence axiom are among many others [34], [53], [58] and [6].

Based on these observations a number of alternative models for the theory of decisions under risk have been developed. An example of such alternatives is the class of rank-dependent expected utility (RDEU) models. Agents maximize an expected utility with respect to a particular transformation of the probabilities of the consequences. Different versions of RDEU models have been proposed and partially axiomatized in [45], [67], [50], [54], [64] and [16]. In addition to these works, analyses of risk attitudes of individuals within the RDEU class have been conducted in [9], [50], [63] and [8]. From a decision theorist's point of view the class of rank-dependent expected utility theories constitutes the most popular generalization of von Neumann and Morgenstern's classic approach. This perception is supported by empirical results in [62], [6] and [21].

The works cited so far have focused on modeling situations involving a single decision-maker. Choices of a rational individual with a given and fixed preference pattern underlie the principle of optimality. This means that the individual's ex-ante well-being only depends on her own choices. Strategic interaction among agents has not yet been considered. Such a type of interaction forms the basis of non-cooperative game theory. Agents take into account that their payoffs do not solely depend on their own action but may also be substantially influenced by the comportment of other individuals. In the context of game theory the uncertainty of each individual therefore results at least partially from strategic risk whereas in the context of decision theory under risk it results from probabilistic risk with known probabilities which cannot be influenced by other agents' behavior. Classic references in non-cooperative game theory are again [39] as well as the textbook [33]. Modern works are amongst many others [19] and [41].

Since the eighties the development of alternative theoretical approaches to the modeling of decision-making under risk has made some significant progress, in particular through the RDEU models. Yet, these newly-developed theories have only been used to a minor degree as the decision-theoretic basis in applications, especially in game theory. Due to the descriptive weaknesses of expected utility theory described in the aforementioned studies this form of modeling appears very desirable. In traditional non-cooperative game theory individuals are assumed, just as in general choice theory, to behave completely rationally and to have an overall understanding for the sometimes outmost complex structure of particular interactions. Recently, numerous experimental works have emphasized that outcomes of games do not correspond to the predictions of those theories which adopt the assumption of unemotional, rational agents. Some critical reflections on game-theoretic concepts can for instance be found in [24]. Approaches which presume bounded rationality and stress procedural aspects in decision-making have been developed. In recent contributions, e.g. [5], theories of learning and limited strategic behavior on the basis of psychological principles have been introduced. Likewise, Gintis has highlighted in [20] evolutionary aspects and the importance of the players' learning behavior. Amongst other works, it has been found in [31] and [7] that individuals do not always behave in a fully self-interested manner but may rather have preferences for fairness, envy or altruism.

The last-mentioned works dispense with the assumption that an agent's sole objective is to maximize her own monetary payoff. Yet, the modeling of the agents as rational individuals who act optimally according to their respective preferences is maintained. In evolutionary game theory this idea is completely abandoned. Instead, an approach is chosen in which randomly and repeatedly drawn boundedly rational or even irrational agents from a large population 'play' a given strategic 'game'. Typically, it is assumed that these agents do not make any decisions about their actions, neither rationally nor suboptimally. They rather follow a genetically preassigned strategy. This strategy is the 'type' of the agent. Here, the exogenously given payoffs do not represent any preferences of the players. In fact, these values are interpreted as objectively measurable 'fitness' which determine the course of evolution. The evolutionary selection process favors those agents whose preprogrammed strategy yields the highest average fitness. By mutation process a small population share of new agents may emerge. The latter agents' strategy is potentially more successful compared to the distribution of strategies in the overall population. The question as to which types may in principle remain or 'survive' in such an environment of interacting agents has been tackled via several theoretical models. The most well-known solution concept in this context is the 'evolutionary stable strategy' (ESS; [37]). It is a static concept which does not explain how a certain population in which all members use a specific strategy is actually reached. Once reached, the population is required to be immune against mutations, in the sense that the incumbents always attain a strictly higher average fitness than any possible mutant could. The related but weaker concept of a 'neutrally stable strategy' (NSS) has also been introduced by Maynard Smith (1982). The requirement of a strictly higher fitness in comparison with the mutants is replaced by a weak inequality here. The most popular explicitly dynamic model in evolutionary game theory is Taylor and Jonker's replicator dynamics ([60]). It requires the population share of a type yielding a higher fitness than another type to increase over time relative to the share of this second type.

A crucial disadvantage of these models is that their fundamental ideas such as the fixed commitment to a specific strategy largely resemble biological principles for less developed organisms. In strong contrast to the approaches which assume full rationality, the cognitive abilities of humans are underrated considerably here. Within the last decade a few contributions to the literature on evolution of preferences have sought to cure this defect. Preferences are now explained endogenously. The works essentially are based on the aforementioned 'indirect evolutionary approach' which originated in the contributions in [23] and [22]. Agents from a large population are matched to play a strategic game with a finite number of pure strategies. Types are now defined as preferences on the set of strategy profiles of the respective game form. In no way these preferences need to coincide with the given fitness. It is assumed that agents behave optimally, in the sense that they always choose the most preferred strategy available according to their

respective preference relation, i.e. their type, given the strategy of their
respective opponent. The choice of a strategy is now carried out as the
result of a rational player's decision process and not due to a fixed ge-
netic commitment. This indirect approach appears more sophisticated
because preferences constitute the very basics of economic behavior and
the choice of a particular strategy should ideally come as a result of a
rational agent's optimal decision. As customary in evolutionary game
theory, the evolutionary 'success' of each agent is determined by its
average fitness, i.e. the material payoff level received in the game. In
the course of evolution types generating low fitness will be driven out
of the population and only agents of types yielding the highest average
fitness will survive. This corresponds to the principle of the 'survival
of the fittest' which is largely attributed to Darwin ([11]). The natural question that arises is whether, using an appropriately adapted
stability concept, types which coincide with the objective fitness necessarily prove to be most successful during the course of evolution. The
idea that other preferences may possibly dominate results from the
supposed observability of preferences and the emerging bindingness for
the respective opponent (cf. [18]). For, the opponent may now choose a
different strategy generating a potential increase in the former agent's
objective fitness. For example, [4], [43] and [57] demonstrate evolutionary advantages of altruism as well as of spite and reciprocal preferences. All these authors yet work with subclasses of preferences which
are adequately adapted to their respective models. In [14], Dekel, Ely
and Yilankaya allow for largely arbitrary preference relations on the
pure strategy profiles of the given game form, but they require agents
to maximize their expected utility in the mixed extension. Because of
the aforementioned shortcomings of the standard choice models, the
former seems indeed to be a desirable property. In particular, an individual may assign different von Neumann-Morgenstern utility values
to two pure strategy profiles that yield identical fitness values. Among
other things the model includes preferences for fairness and altruism.
However, due to the limitations of the independence axiom the second
assumption appears very unattractive. It does not seem reasonable that
decision-makers in such an environment should necessarily maximize
an expected utility. In a related paper, Ely and Yilankaya themselves
question the appropriateness of this assumption ("We do not mean
to advance to the position that rationality implies an expected utility
representation of preferences", [17], p. 257). It rather seems that the
assumption has been made in order to simplify the analysis. Moreover,
each utility function on the set of strategy profiles with values in a

fixed compact interval is identified in [14] with a different type. Yet, each preference relation allows for a continuum of such utility representations. A specific preference relation is thus embodied in the model by an infinite number of different types. This assumption simplifies a number of steps in some proofs substantially. It is economically not very reasonable though since distinct types should represent agents with different elementary characteristics. In [14] two agents of distinct types may be completely indistinguishable in this respect.

An essential question that we are going further into within this work concerns the findings from a general evolutionary model of the endogenous determination of preferences including the non-expected utility case. First of all, we formulate a mathematically rigorous model without restrictions and less appealing assumptions such as the multiple embedding of identical preferences through pretendedly different types. Several basic components, in particular the structure of the matching process, the solution concept and some proofs are based on the model in [14]. As in the literature on evolutionary game theory and on the evolution of preferences we assume that agents from a single large set are matched. Here, they play the mixed extension of a strategic game with a finite number of pure strategies and exogenous fitness values. A type shall represent a preference relation on the set of mixed strategy profiles. We assume that the outcome of such a game of any two agents is always a Nash equilibrium according to the two agents' preferences. In order to assure existence of such an equilibrium, certain minimal requirements on preferences, namely continuity and some form of convexity on the set of own strategies, remain necessary. Yet, these appear to be significantly weaker than expected utility maximization.

In this work, we concentrate on a purely static analysis. Applying the stability concept introduced in [14], we study the properties of evolutionary stable populations where a population is a probability distribution over types with a finite support. A population is said to be stable if all agents of types which are elements of the population's support receive the same average fitness and if no mutant can enter that population with the agents of this type receiving a strictly higher average fitness than any agent of an incumbent type. This concept is in the same spirit as Maynard Smith's 'neutrally stable strategy' (NSS; [36]) described above. Our analysis includes the question as to whether the outcome of a match of any agents of types from a stable population must necessarily correspond to a Nash equilibrium of the material game, i.e. the game in which both players maximize their expected fitness. For non-observable preferences an affirmative answer has been given in [40] and [17]. Hence, we assume that in each match the preference relation of the respective opponent is fully observable. Justifications for assuming observability are provided in [22] and [18]. Moreover, if preferences were not observable, every agent would only face the same distribution of opponents' actions with no other information being given. Hence, there is no advantage in having non-standard preferences since no opponent can ever observe them. Obviously, preferences that maximize true fitness should perform best in the evolutionary sense. In the case of perceptability other results are a priori possible because of the mentioned commitment effect. Indeed, we are able to formally confirm this guess. Consider, for instance, a situation in which the fitness values are given by the payoffs in a prisoner's dilemma. Non-cooperation (also referred to as 'defection'), the natural Nash equilibrium strategy, is not required to be chosen in a stable population. We prove a force towards efficient pairs of strategies, similar to Robson's 'secret handshake' ([47]). Efficiency of a strategy here means that no other strategy can yield a strictly higher expected fitness when played against itself.

A second fundamental and important question concerns the existence of evolutionary stable populations. In this regard, even the most established solution concepts in evolutionary game theory have considerable weaknesses. Many games fail to have an evolutionary stable strategy (ESS) and Taylor and Jonker's replicator dynamics ([60]) do not necessarily converge outside the class of models with two players and two pure strategies. Above all, in Dekel et al.'s approach on the evolution of preferences ([14]) a stable population does not even exist for generic 2×2 games. Existence is merely warranted in a subclass and the authors make no statement about the case with an arbitrary finite number of pure strategies. An important aim of our work is to develop a model in which such a stable population can always be obtained. Indeed, we prove existence for any finite number of pure strategies in our setup with very general preferences. Furthermore, the robustness of this result with respect to an important specification of the type space is shown for the 2×2 case. More precisely, this means that existence can be maintained when imposing some form of betweenness in addition to continuity. This is an important finding since betweenness is significantly stronger than our previous requirements and constitutes a step back towards Dekel et al.'s expected utility assumption ([14]). Yet, a model with betweenness is, just as the RDEU models, an intuitive weakening and alternative to von Neumann and Morgenstern's theory ([39]). In particular, the main paradoxes of expected utility theory may still be explained in such an environment.

Further, we analyze which preferences may be elements of the support of a stable population and which may not. This question is especially interesting since evolutionary justifications for expected utility maximizing behavior have been given in several articles, e.g. in [29], [10] and [48]. However, in these works it is assumed that preferences arise from situations with a single decision-maker. Strategic interaction as in our approach has not been considered. A comparison of the consequences appears very promising most notably because of the above-mentioned commitment effect for the opponent. As a matter of fact, non-expected utility preferences may turn out to have evolutionary advantages over expected utility preferences. We demonstrate that for 2×2 games with generic fitness no stable population may ever contain a type which has an expected utility representation.

Finally, we conclude the work with an overview and outlook, in particular with respect to an extension of the model to a setup with two populations. For each match the two agents are drawn according to different populations. It turns out that this assumption has some minor impact on the results, but most of our earlier findings prove to be robust to such an extension. The tendency towards some efficient strategy profile as in the model with a single population still occurs. Yet, the previous efficiency concept is not adequate in this setup. Furthermore, we show that evolution still need not select Nash equilibria of the material game.

The book is structured as follows. In Chap. 2 we begin with a short review of some concepts from the theory of choice and non-cooperative game theory. We then introduce the main model, initially describing the nature of the interaction, the participating agents and the possible types. After a description of the matching process and the determination of each agent's evolutionary fitness, we present the stability concept for populations as well as the concept of efficiency of a strategy. The main result of the chapter establishes existence of a stable population for any number of pure strategies and for an arbitrary fitness function. We illustrate these findings in Chap. 3 with two examples in which the fitness values resemble the well-known prisoner's dilemma and a coordination game situation. Furthermore, we discuss the model's ability to include specific alternative models of decision-making under risk such as the RDEU models. Chap. 4 focuses on the special case with two pure strategies, i.e. where the interaction is a 2×2 game. We demonstrate that for generic fitness values preferences which differ from those having an expected utility representation indeed have evolutionary advantages. More precisely, the support of a stable population does typically not include any type which is represented by an expected utility. We subsequently examine the specific preference relations which may actually be part of a stable population in this case. In Chap. 5 we stick to the 2×2 case and explore whether more structure on our previous type space still allows to maintain existence of a stable population. For this purpose, we require preferences to satisfy betweenness on the own strategy space in addition to continuity. The type space is now smaller but still comprises preferences that correspond to an important weakening of expected utility theory. As it turns out, we obtain an affirmative answer concerning the question of existence. Finally, Chap. 6 highlights the importance of a couple of assumptions made in the previous model. In particular, we discuss the influence of the fact that any two agents which interact with each other are drawn according to a single population. We emphasize that some of the earlier results depend on this assumption. In Chap. 7 we gather results and conclude. All lengthy proofs are placed in the Appendix in order to support the clearness of the exposition.

2

The Model and a General Existence Result

Literature that investigates evolutionary models of economic behavior usually takes as primitive a given strategic game. Yet, the 'payoffs' are material: They do not represent utilities of the potential players as in the formal definition of a game, but are rather interpreted as biological fitness. In our model, agents of types from a population, where a type is a preference relation on the strategy profiles, are matched in pairs to interact with each other in this strategic environment, i.e. they play a game that has the same strategy sets as the material game. It is assumed that in each match a Nash equilibrium according to the two players' preferences is played. The agents' reproductive or evolutionary success is determined by the fitness that they receive from these interactions. A population is said to be stable if all its members induce the same average fitness and if the population is immune to successful invasions through mutation. A mutant is a preference relation from the type space which enters the population in a small fraction. With immunity we mean that no such 'entrant' type may be able to generate a strictly higher average fitness in the post-entry population than any of the 'incumbent' types.

The main focus of this chapter is on the existence of stable populations. This is an especially interesting issue since our main contribution compared to previous models on the evolution of preferences is the generality of the type space. We solely impose two very weak restrictions on its elements, continuity and a convexity condition. This is far less than the commonly used assumption that preferences on mixed strategy profiles admit an expected utility representation. In evolutionary models existence is always a crucial issue and many such models fail to create a stable population. The main result of this chapter is that in our model such a stable population always exists. For every material fitness and any finite number of pure strategies there is a population of types which cannot be successfully invaded by any mutant.

In Sect. 2.1 we briefly review some elements from non-cooperative game theory and choice under risk. The material game and the type space are formally described in Sect. 2.2 using the concept of a strategic preform, followed by a discussion of the matching process and the resulting average fitness for each agent in Sect. 2.3. The stability concept is introduced in Sect. 2.4, where we also describe the relation of stability to the concept of efficiency of a strategy. Finally, in Sect. 2.5, we state our main existence theorem.

2.1 Preliminaries

In this section we introduce some basic terminology and recall a couple of essential definitions. We begin with the concepts of a preference relation and a utility function in Subsect. 2.1.1, followed by an introduction to strategic games and the most familiar solution concept, Nash equilibrium, in Subsect. 2.1.2. These definitions should be well-known elements from basic choice theory and non-cooperative game theory. The formal background is recalled primarily since there are significant differences across the literature in this regard. We will apply the ideas as primal components in our model which we describe in the next section.

2.1.1 Preferences and Utility

Let Z be a non-empty set describing alternatives among which an individual (or an 'agent') can choose. A binary relation on Z may allow for pairwise comparisons of alternatives, i.e. elements of Z. If such a binary relation satisfies the completeness and transitivity axioms, it is called a preference relation on Z.

Definition 2.1. *A preference relation $\succsim$ on Z is a binary relation on Z with the following two properties:*

i. *Completeness: For all $z_1, z_2 \in Z$ we have $z_1 \succsim z_2$ or $z_2 \succsim z_1$,*
ii. *Transitivity: For all $z_1, z_2, z_3 \in Z$, if $z_1 \succsim z_2$ and $z_2 \succsim z_3$ hold, then we have $z_1 \succsim z_3$.*

Definition 2.1 is most commonly used in the literature. However, some authors just define a preference relation as a binary relation on the set of alternatives. Completeness and transitivity are then additionally required as the 'weak order axioms'. Here and there, a third axiom, called 'reflexivity', is imposed. It asks for every alternative to be preferred to itself. In fact, reflexivity is immediately implied by completeness.

The strict preference and the indifference relation are defined as customary.

Definition 2.2. *Let $\succsim$ be a preference relation on Z.*

i.   The strict preference $\succ$ on Z is defined by

$$z_1 \succ z_2 :\Longleftrightarrow z_1 \succsim z_2 \text{ but not } z_2 \succsim z_1. \tag{2.1}$$

ii. The indifference relation $\sim$ on Z is defined by

$$z_1 \sim z_2 :\Longleftrightarrow z_1 \succsim z_2 \text{ and } z_2 \succsim z_1. \tag{2.2}$$

We read $z \succsim z'$ as 'z is preferred to z'', further $z \succ z'$ as 'z is strictly preferred to z'', and $z \sim z'$ as 'the agent is indifferent between z and z''. Note that neither the strict preference nor the indifference relation is a preference relation according to Definition 2.1. The completeness axiom is not fulfilled in either case.

We continue with a recapitulation of the concept of a utility representation of a preference relation.

Definition 2.3. *Let $\succsim$ be a preference relation on Z. A function $u : Z \to \mathbb{R}$ represents $\succsim$ if for any z_1, $z_2 \in Z$ we have*

$$z_1 \succsim z_2 \Longleftrightarrow u(z_1) \geq u(z_2). \tag{2.3}$$

The function u is called an (ordinal) utility function representing $\succsim$.

The next definition provides a continuity requirement for preference relations which turns out to be sufficient to guarantee the existence of a representing continuous utility function.

Definition 2.4. *Let Z be a topological space. A preference relation $\succsim$ on Z is said to be continuous if for any $z \in Z$ the sets $\{ y \in Z \mid y \succsim z \}$ and $\{ y \in Z \mid z \succsim y \}$ are closed.*

This is just one of many definitions of continuity of preferences. For instance, we could have required the sets $\{ y \in Z \mid y \succ z \}$ and $\{ y \in Z \mid z \succ y \}$ to be open.

With some minor assumptions on the structure of the set of alternatives we obtain Debreu's theorem. It states that under these conditions every continuous preference relation on a set of alternatives can be represented by a continuous utility function.

Theorem 2.5 ([12]). *Let Z be a topological space with a countable base of open sets. Further, let $\succsim$ be a continuous preference relation on Z. Then, there exists a continuous utility function that represents $\succsim$.*

All preference relations that we discuss in the remainder of this work will be assumed to satisfy continuity in order to assure a utility representation. We like to remind that this representation is not unique. Any strictly monotone transformation of a utility function representing a preference relation yields another function which represents the same preferences. We omit the details and refer to the standard textbook literature on microeconomic theory.

2.1.2 Strategic Games

In this subsection we recall the concepts of a strategic preform and a strategic game. Proper mathematical definitions are especially important as we will study how preferences on strategy profiles of a given preform might evolve over time. The latter procedure is formally described in the next sections. The exposition here is restricted to environments with two players since such a setup will form the basis of our evolutionary model.

Definition 2.6. *A two-player strategic preform is a pair $(N, (S_i)_{i \in N})$ consisting of*

i. a set of players N with $|N| = 2$,
ii. a pair $(S_i)_{i \in N}$ of non-empty sets S_i, $i \in N$.

The set S_i is called player i's strategy set. The set $\bar{S} \equiv \Pi_{i \in N} S_i$ is called the set of strategy profiles.

A two-player strategic game is readily defined when a strategic preform as in Definition 2.6 is combined with a preference relation on the set of strategy profiles for either player.

Definition 2.7. *A two-player strategic game is a 3-tupel $(N, (S_i)_{i \in N}, (\succsim_i)_{i \in N})$ consisting of*

i. a set of players N with $|N| = 2$,
ii. a pair $(S_i)_{i \in N}$ of non-empty sets S_i, $i \in N$,
iii. a pair $(\succsim_i)_{i \in N}$ of preference relations $\succsim_i$ on $S_i \times S_{-i}$, $i \in N$.

Note that Definition 2.7 is more general than the definitions given in most introductions to non-cooperative game theory. Frequently, the preference relations in condition *iii.* are substituted by a pair of utility functions on the set of strategy profiles, one for each player. The utility values are, in the context of games, usually referred to as 'payoffs'. Under the assumption that the preferences are continuous both requirements are equivalent (cf. Theorem 2.5) as long as each S_i has the necessary topological structure. However, as our main interest is in the evolution of preferences, preferences seem to be the more appropriate primitives. We will discuss this issue more extensively later. Remarkably, even in the literature on the evolution of preferences most authors prefer to work with utility functions rather than with true preference relations.

Next, we give a definition of convexity of preferences on the set of strategy profiles of a two-player strategic game.

Definition 2.8. *Let S_i and S_{-i} be non-empty, convex subsets of some Euclidean space. A preference relation $\succsim_i$ on $S_i \times S_{-i}$ is convex on S_i if for every $s^* \in S_i \times S_{-i}$ the set $\{s_i \in S_i : (s_i, s^*_{-i}) \succsim_i s^*\}$ is convex.*

The condition in Definition 2.8 will be prevalently referred to as 'convexity on the own strategy set' or 'convexity in the first component'. It says that, given any strategy profile, the subset of own strategies that one could choose such that the new profile (with the chosen own strategy and the strategy of the opponent as before) is preferred to the given profile needs to be convex. In the main model of this work all players have identical strategy sets. With the terminology 'convexity on the own strategy set' any unclarity should be avoided.

Note that we could have stated Definition 2.8 already in Sect. 2.1.1. For, in principle, the concept can be used outside the framework of strategic games. Yet, in this work it will be applied in the latter way only, i.e. with S_i and S_{-i} interpreted as the strategy sets of the agent (whose preference relation $\succsim_i$ is described) and her opponent, respectively.

It will be convenient to work with the best-response correspondence induced by a preference relation on strategy profiles.

Definition 2.9. *Let $\succsim_i$ be a preference relation on $S_i \times S_{-i}$. The multivalued function $\beta_i : S_{-i} \Rightarrow S_i$ defined by*

$$\beta_i(s_{-i}) = \{s_i \in S_i \mid (s_i, s_{-i}) \succsim_i (s'_i, s_{-i}) \text{ for all } s'_i \in S_i\} \qquad (2.4)$$

is called i's best-response correspondence.

For any fixed strategy of the opponent the best-response correspondence in the sense of Definition 2.9 specifies a subset of the agent's strategies such that the resulting profiles (with the given strategy of the opponent) are most preferred (or 'optimal') according to her preferences. In order for this to be a meaningful concept, we need to assume 'rational' behavior of the agent in the sense that she always chooses an available alternative which is best according to her preference relation.

A strategy profile in a two-player strategic game which is such that either player's respective strategy is optimal given the opponent's strategy, i.e. a best response, is called a Nash equilibrium of the game.

Definition 2.10. *Let* $(N, (S_i)_{i \in N}, (\succsim_i)_{i \in N})$ *be a two-player strategic game. A strategy profile* $s^{NE} \in \Pi_{i \in N} S_i$ *is a Nash equilibrium of the game if for both* $i \in N$ *we have* $s_i^{NE} \in \beta_i(s_{-i}^{NE})$.

The following theorem specifies sufficient conditions for the existence of such a Nash equilibrium in a two-person strategic game. Its proof is based on Kakutani's fixed point theorem ([28]). The current two-player version of the result is slightly more general than Nash's existence theorem ([38]) because the latter deals with (expected) payoff functions instead of the underlying preference relations.

Lemma 2.11. *Let* $(N, (S_i)_{i \in N}, (\succsim_i)_{i \in N})$ *be a two-player strategic game. Suppose that for both* $i \in N$ *we have that*

i. S_i *is a non-empty, compact, and convex subset of some Euclidean space,*

ii. $\succsim_i$ *is continuous on* $S_i \times S_{-i}$ *and convex on* S_i.

Then, the strategic game has a Nash equilibrium.

Next, we consider the special case in which the two players' strategy sets coincide, i.e. there exists some S such that for both $i \in N$ we have $S_i = S$. This case meets economic habits; the strategy sets yet receive an additional intrinsic meaning. It should be well understood that any sort of invariance with respect to permutations of some player's strategies gets lost. A preference relation $\succsim_i$ is hence now defined on $S \times S$. Unless stated otherwise and as before, the first component in this Cartesian product shall represent i's own strategy set, the second component is the strategy set of the opponent.

The next result says that, under the conditions of Lemma 2.11, every two-player strategic game, in which both players have identical strategy sets and preferences, i.e. where the characteristics of the two players are identical except for their 'names', has a 'symmetric' Nash equilibrium.

Lemma 2.12. *Let $(N, (S, S), (\succsim, \succsim))$ be a two-player strategic game. Suppose that*

i. S is a non-empty, compact, and convex subset of a Euclidian vector space,

ii. $\succsim$ is continuous on $S \times S$ and convex on the own strategy set.

Then, there exists an $s^{SN} \in S$ such that (s^{SN}, s^{SN}) is a Nash equilibrium. Such a strategy profile is called a symmetric Nash equilibrium.

Just as for the previous result, the proof of Lemma 2.12 is based on Kakutani's fixed point theorem ([28]). For a detailed introduction to the Nash equilibrium concept and existence issues we refer to graduate-level textbooks on non-cooperative game theory. A commendable review dealing with preference relations instead of commonly used payoffs is given in [41].

2.2 Interaction, Fitness and Individual Preferences

We now have all prerequisites and are able to introduce the formal model underlying the analysis of the evolution of preferences that we will undertake in the remainder of this work. We begin with a description of the interaction of agents of different types. The idea is that agents from a large set, with typically heterogeneous preferences, are randomly and repeatedly matched to play a strategic game. This environment is described by a strategic preform specifying the set of strategies that each agent drawn to play has at her disposal. Second, a 'fitness function' determines the material payoffs, or the evolutionary success, for each outcome of the interaction, i.e. for each strategy profile.

The preferences of the agents, so-called types, may differ from the material payoffs. The composition of these types is characterized by a probability distribution (a 'population') on a type space which underlies only some very weak restrictions.

2.2.1 Strategic Preform and Fitness Function

Formally, we consider a two-player strategic preform $(N, (\Delta^n, \Delta^n))$, where Δ^n is the unit simplex in $\mathbb{R}^n$:

$$\Delta^n \equiv \big\{(\sigma^1, ..., \sigma^n) \in \mathbb{R}^n \mid$$
$$\sigma^i \geq 0 \text{ for all } i = 1, ..., n \text{ and } \sum_{i=1}^{n} \sigma^i = 1\big\}. \tag{2.5}$$

The interpretation is that we have some finite set of 'pure strategies', $\bar{A} = \{a_1, ..., a_n\}$, and take as the strategy set for each player the set of 'mixed strategies', Δ^n, which is the set of probability distributions over $\bar{A}$. Hence, when choosing a mixed strategy $\sigma = (\sigma^1, ..., \sigma^n)$ in Δ^n, an agent randomizes among the pure strategies and plays the pure strategy $a_j \in \bar{A}$ with probability σ^j. We will identify a_i with the ith unit vector in $\mathbb{R}^n$, i.e. with the element e_i of Δ^n. We are aware that one could go along without the set $\bar{A}$ and more generally treat Δ^n as each agent's strategy set, without its interpretation as mixed strategies. The fitness function π as below would then directly be defined as in (2.6) with each $\pi(a_i, a_j)$, $i, j \in \{1, ..., n\}$, just being some real number π_{ij}. However, for ease of exposition we will mainly stick to the terminology 'mixed strategy' although it would be very well possible to dispense with it.

Furthermore, we assume the existence of a function $\pi : \bar{A} \times \bar{A} \to \mathbb{R}$ defined on the set of pure strategy profiles. Its values are assumed to represent biological 'fitness' in such a manner that for each $i \in N$ the value $\pi(a, a')$ is the fitness that player i receives if she is playing the pure strategy a and her opponent is playing a'. The term 'fitness' should refer to some kind of evolutionary strength like probability of survival or expected number of offspring. We refer to the introduction for a detailed discussion of this concept. The fitness function is defined on $\bar{A} \times \bar{A}$ in order to reflect the assumption that each individual has finitely many pure choices available in every interaction with other agents. As to randomizations, we assume that π can be extended (using the same terminology π) to the domain of mixed strategy profiles, i.e. to $\Delta^n \times \Delta^n$, by taking expected values:

$$\pi(\sigma, \sigma') \equiv \sum_{i=1}^{n} \sum_{j=1}^{n} \sigma^i \, \sigma'^j \, \pi(a_i, a_j) \quad \text{for } (\sigma, \sigma') \in \Delta^n \times \Delta^n. \quad (2.6)$$

Hence, player i's expected fitness from a strategy profile (σ_i, σ_{-i}) in $\Delta^n \times \Delta^n$ is given by $\pi(\sigma_i, \sigma_{-i})$. As we will see shortly, the evolutionary success of an agent in terms of the population share of its type in a generally polymorphic population depends on the fitness values the agent receives from playing strategic games with preform $(N, (\Delta^n, \Delta^n))$ with other agents from that population. Note that the function π determines each individual's fitness in all these interactions. It is independent of the type of an agent and her opponent and also irrespective of the names of the two players in the game. Thus, we say that the fitness function or the 'game' is 'symmetric'.

In virtually all of the literature on evolutionary game theory or on evolution of preferences this situation is referred to as a "symmetric game". The fitness values are commonly referred to as the 'true' or 'material payoffs' of the game. Intuitively, the idea behind this is clear. However, formally we like to emphasize that a strategic game is solely determined by the given preform and the players' preferences (see Definition 2.7). Any 'payoffs' should be regarded as utilities with respect to these preferences. Generally, the fitness values may be completely unrelated to the respective game that is played by any two agents of types from the population. Their preference relations (or, more formally, the representing utility functions) need a priori not be 'close' to the fitness function in any sense. The latter just determines the evolutionary success of each agent in any match and consequently the composition of types, as we will see in the next section. Therefore, the symmetry property here is really limited to all agents of all types being evaluated by the same fitness function. A precise definition of symmetries (via motions of a game) in a game is given in [42]. Note that our setup doubtlessly excludes a number of material games which are in fact symmetric according to the cited work.

Example 2.13. Table 2.1 is a graphical representation of symmetric fitness values according to our modeling above given a two-player strategic preform with two pure strategies, i.e. with $n = 2$ and $\bar{A} = \{A, B\}$.

Table 2.1. Symmetric Fitness Values

	A	B
A	a,a	b,c
B	c,b	d,d

We have set $a \equiv \pi(A, A)$, $b \equiv \pi(A, B)$, $c \equiv \pi(B, A)$ and $d \equiv \pi(B, B)$. The strategy sets of the two players are given by Δ^2, the set of probability distributions on $\{A, B\}$. The fitness values for mixed strategy profiles in $\Delta^2 \times \Delta^2$ can be computed according to (2.6).

It is important to reemphasize that the matrix in Example 2.13 indicates only the fitness values that the agents may obtain from the matches to be specified in the next section. As mentioned before, these values have, in principle, nothing to do with the preferences on strategy profiles that any agent possesses. However, the fitness values will determine the evolutionary success generated by each type in the population.

2.2.2 The Population

We have introduced the basic characteristics of the interaction, i.e. a strategic preform with two players and the same set of mixed strategies for the players. In order to obtain a strategic game according to Definition 2.7 we need to complete the description by adding the two preference relations on strategy profiles.

The idea is that a population consists of multiple types, where a type is identified with a preference relation on the set of strategy profiles of the given preform, $\Delta^n \times \Delta^n$. Agents with preferences according to this population are randomly and repeatedly matched in pairs. Each pair plays the strategic game which is readily defined by the strategic preform from Sect. 2.2.1 and the preference relations of the two agents.

When considering a preference relation on $\Delta^n \times \Delta^n$, the first component in this Cartesian product represents such an agent's own strategy set, the second component is the strategy set of the opponent. This implies that a preference relation is independent of the type of the opponent. Basically, we like to allow for all preference relations on the set of strategy profiles to possibly occur in a population. However, for technical reasons and tractability, we need to assume that these preferences are continuous and satisfy convexity on the set of own strategies.

Definition 2.14. *Let $(N, (\Delta^n, \Delta^n))$ be a two-player strategic preform. The type space, denoted by $\mathcal{T}$, is the set of all preference relations on $\Delta^n \times \Delta^n$ which are convex in the first component and continuous.*

The restrictions on this type space are in line with the most fundamental assumptions commonly imposed on preference relations. As in Theorem 2.5, continuity essentially assures the existence of a continuous utility function. The convexity requirement guarantees the existence of a Nash equilibrium in every game played by two agents of types from $\mathcal{T}$ as we will see shortly. Note that a Nash equilibrium of such a game need not at all be a Nash equilibrium of the game in which the players' preferences are represented by the fitness function. We follow other authors and refer occasionally to the latter game as the 'material payoffs game'. Also note that we have not indexed the type space $\mathcal{T}$ by the number n of pure strategies. As n changes we clearly get a different type space.

Our requirements are significantly weaker than those typically imposed in models on the evolution of preferences. In a closely related work, [14], agents with arbitrary preferences on the set of pure strategy profiles of a given preform are allowed for. However, the authors assume that the preferences satisfy the axioms of expected utility theory in the mixed extension. That is, for any agent of type T from their type space, there exists a von Neumann-Morgenstern utility function $u_T : \bar{A} \times \bar{A} \to [0,1]$ such that for any $\sigma_T, \sigma'_T, \sigma_{-T}, \sigma'_{-T} \in \Delta^n$ the preference pattern $(\sigma_T, \sigma_{-T}) \succsim_T (\sigma'_T, \sigma'_{-T})$ holds if and only if $\sum_i \sum_j \sigma_T^i \sigma_{-T}^j u_T(a_i, a_j) \geq \sum_i \sum_j \sigma_T'^i \sigma_{-T}'^j u_T(a_i, a_j)$. Henceforth, the notation T will be used as a synonym for the preference relation $\succsim_T$. As discussed in the introduction, the possibility of preferences which differ from objective fitness seems to be a desirable feature given the empirical evidence that people do not always behave in a pure self-interested manner. However, it seems rather implausible that such agents necessarily maximize an expected utility when comparing risky alternatives, in particular with regard to the numerous observations on the violation of the independence axiom of the theory of choice under risk.

A second undesirable feature of the cited work is that each such utility function in expected utility form is identified with a different type. In particular, this implies that two functions on $\Delta^n \times \Delta^n$ which are positive affine transformations of each other, e.g., $u_1 \equiv 0$ and $u_2 \equiv 0.1$, characterize two distinct types. However, the two functions represent the same preference relation, i.e. the two types are economically identical. In the present model this weakness does not occur.

We continue with the definition of a population.

Definition 2.15. *Let $(N, (\Delta^n, \Delta^n))$ be a two-player strategic preform. A population is a function $\mu : \mathcal{T} \to [0,1]$ such that the following conditions are satisfied:*

i. $C(\mu) \equiv \{T \in \mathcal{T} \mid \mu(T) > 0\}$ *is finite,*
ii. $\sum_{T \in C(\mu)} \mu(T) = 1$.

The set of all populations is denoted by $\mathcal{P}(\mathcal{T})$.

We interpret $\mu(T)$ as the population share of type $T \in \mathcal{T}$. It is the probability that a randomly drawn agent according to population μ is of type T. The set $C(\mu)$ will be referred to as the support of μ. In a slight abuse of terminology, we will occasionally call a population according to Definition 2.15 a probability distribution on $\mathcal{T}$. The assumption that such a function has a finite support shall reflect the idea that the set of agents is large but there are only finitely many different types for these agents. Finiteness enhances the presentability of the model by avoiding unreasonably complex situations. It allows us to focus on the question of whether any lasting ('stable') population will emerge under evolutionary pressures and, if so, which properties such a population may have.

At this point, we like to remark that some specific modern alternatives to von Neumann and Morgenstern's expected utility theory ([39]) do not satisfy the convexity requirement that we impose on our type space $\mathcal{T}$ in Definition 2.14. However, with such preferences the resulting game of two agents could fail to have a Nash equilibrium. Hence, if one wishes to further generalize the model in order to include such preferences, other concepts for the outcome of a match between two agents will be needed. Such a model could be a potential for future research. We further elaborate on this issue in Sect. 3.3.

2.3 Matching Process and Evolutionary Fitness

In this section we discuss how agents of different types from a given population interact with each other and how the fitness function determines the evolutionary success of agents of each type.

We assume that preferences are fully observable. This means that whenever an agent is drawn to interact with some other agent she is able to recognize the type of her opponent. Consequently, the resulting game is of complete information. The preference relations on the set of strategy profiles are known to the participating players.

Assuming full observability of preferences is certainly restrictive. Yet, it is in line with a number of works that adopt the indirect evolutionary approach, in particular with the early contributions [23] and [22]. Besides, several authors, such as in [40] and [17], have analyzed models in which preferences are unobservable. In these papers the agents merely know the distribution of types in the population. The main finding is that the aggregate play in this population must necessarily coincide with a Nash equilibrium of the game with expected fitness maximizing players, i.e. the material payoffs game. The reason is that preferences different from the given fitness have no strategic advantage if no opponent can observe them. A commitment effect does not occur. In addition, in [22] it is pointed out that for some of the results incidental rather then full observability of preferences is sufficient. It is argued that it would be likewise restrictive to assume their complete unobservability. In this regard, certain human reactions and behavior such as emotions and anger are referred to in [18]. Because of the occurrence of these symptoms, a human may never be able to entirely disclose her true preferences.

Note that, whenever two agents are drawn according to a population of types from $\mathcal{T}$, the resulting game must necessarily have a Nash equilibrium. This is due to our two structural assumptions, continuity

and convexity on the own strategy set of the preference relations that
we have imposed on the type space $\mathcal{T}$. Existence follows immediately
from Lemma 2.11.

Proposition 2.16. *For any two types* $T, T' \in \mathcal{T}$ *the resulting two-player strategic game* $(N, (\Delta^n, \Delta^n), (\succsim_T, \succsim_{T'}))$ *has a Nash equilibrium.*

As to the matching process, we will assume analogously to a treatment in [14] that any two drawn agents play such a Nash equilibrium of
the resulting game. Also, all agents of a specific type behave identically.
That is, if an agent of type T is characterized by a best-response correspondence β_T and she is matched with an agent of type T', then
a strategy profile $(\sigma_T, \sigma_{T'})$ is played such that $\sigma_T \in \beta_T(\sigma_{T'})$ and
$\sigma_{T'} \in \beta_{T'}(\sigma_T)$. In particular, the realized Nash equilibrium will be
the same in all matches of agents of two specific types.

An economic justification for this assumption is that evolution op-
erates very slowly. Thus, Nash equilibrium play can be interpreted as
the outcome of a learning process which runs infinitely faster than the
evolutionary process that underlies our model. An explicit modeling
of a learning process within the general framework of [14] is provided
in [44]. The two analyses lead to equal qualitative results, though. Another work which includes learning to behave according to one's preferences in an explicit dynamic evolutionary model is [51]. The learning
process can be assumed to lead to Nash equilibrium play before the
next evolutionary changes occur. This position is supported by Selten
in [56] where he identifies a hierarchy of dynamic processes and argues
in favor of an adiabatic approximation. This means that whenever a
specific process is analyzed any quicker process "can be assumed to
reach equilibrium instantly" ([56], p. 21).

We continue with the definition of an equilibrium configuration.
Given a population μ, it specifies for any pair of types from $C(\mu)$ the
Nash equilibrium profile played in all the matches of agents of these two
types. This is senseful since a Nash equilibrium need certainly not be
unique. In the case of multiple equilibria, the realized Nash equilibrium
is specified through the equilibrium configuration.

Definition 2.17. *Let* μ *be a population with support* $C(\mu)$. *A family*
$(b_T)_{T \in C(\mu)}$ *of functions* $b_T : C(\mu) \to \Delta^n$, $T \in C(\mu)$, *is called an*
equilibrium configuration if for any $T', T'' \in C(\mu)$ *the strategy pro-*
file $(b_{T'}(T''), b_{T''}(T'))$ *is a Nash equilibrium of the two-player strategic*
game $(N, (\Delta^n, \Delta^n), (\succsim_{T'}, \succsim_{T''}))$.

We denote the set of all possible equilibrium configurations given
μ by $B(\mu)$. For the purpose of keeping some expressions plain we

will sometimes suppress the indices and abbreviate a typical element $(b_T)_{T \in C(\mu)}$ of $B(\mu)$ by b. In order to accentuate its meaning as a strategy we will also occasionally denote $b_T(T')$ by $\sigma^b_{TT'}$. It is the (equilibrium) mixed strategy chosen by an agent of type T when matched with an agent of type T' under the equilibrium configuration $b = (b_T)_{T \in C(\mu)}$.

Definition 2.17 formally reflects our assumption that all agents of the same type (all 'replicas' so to speak) behave identically. In all matches of two agents, say of types T' and T'', these agents always play the same Nash equilibrium $(b_{T'}(T''), b_{T''}(T'))$. Every agent observes the type of her opponent and chooses her strategy on the basis of this observation. In particular, only the type of the opponent is relevant for this choice. In the common representation of a two-player strategic game with n pure strategies as an $n \times n$ matrix this implies that the equilibrium choice does not depend on who is the row or the column player, i.e. the Nash equilibrium that is played is invariant to name changes of the players. This property is reasonable because the evolutionary performance of all agents of all types is evaluated by the same fitness function. In particular, an important implication is that, when two players of the same type are matched, they need to play a symmetric Nash equilibrium. By Lemma 2.12, such a symmetric Nash equilibrium necessarily exists.

Proposition 2.18. *Let* $T \in \mathcal{T}$. *The two-player strategic game* $(N, (\Delta^n, \Delta^n), (\succsim_T, \succsim_T))$ *has a symmetric Nash equilibrium, i.e. there exists* $\sigma_T^{SN} \in \Delta^n$ *such that* $(\sigma_T^{SN}, \sigma_T^{SN})$ *is a Nash equilibrium.*

Given a population of types, μ, and an equilibrium configuration $b = (b_T)_{T \in C(\mu)} \in B(\mu)$, we can compute the average fitness for any agent of type $T \in C(\mu)$. It is given by

$$\Pi_T(\mu \mid b) \equiv \sum_{T' \in C(\mu)} \mu(T')\, \pi(b_T(T'), b_{T'}(T)). \qquad (2.7)$$

This average fitness determines the evolutionary success of each type as we will see in the next section. The choice of an expectation as a selection criterion seems adequate as we imagine matches in an infinite set of agents characterized by a population consisting of finitely many different types to occur infinitely often and the two agents for each match to be drawn independently according to μ. As a consequence of the strong law of large numbers, the fitness will almost surely coincide with the value given on the right-hand side in (2.7).

2.4 Stability Concept and Efficient Strategies

In the previous two sections we have introduced the setup for our analysis of the evolution of preferences. More precisely, we have formally described the basic environment and a population of types where agents with these preferences interact within this environment. Now, we come to the solution concept for our study, a stability criterion for pairs of populations and equilibrium configurations. The implicit idea is that a dynamic process models the evolutionary changes in the composition of the population. Evolution selects successful types in the sense that the population share of a type generating high average fitness as in (2.7) increases relative to the share of those types inducing lower average fitness.

The selection process of an evolutionary model is integrated here by means of a static stability criterion which requires a population to be immune against successful mutations, with a single mutation at a time. A mutation occurs when a type with comparatively small population share enters. Such a 'mutant' shall not be able to generate a higher average fitness in the matches of agents according to the post-entry population than any of the 'incumbent types', i.e. the types that were in the population prior to the entry of the new type. We assume that after the entry the incumbent-type agents continue to play the same Nash equilibria as before when matched among each other. For, there is no reason to presume that changes concerning a small fraction should have any impact on the behavior of the remaining agents. However, the mutant-type agents are typically new in the population. Thus, they have no previous experience and all respective Nash equilibria could possibly occur in the matches of agents of this type with themselves as well as with incumbent-type agents. The stability concept introduced in the following definition checks immunity against every such Nash equilibrium.

We use δ_T to denote a degenerate distribution, i.e. a monomorphic population consisting exclusively of Ts.

Definition 2.19. *Let* $\pi : \bar{A} \times \bar{A} \to \mathbb{R}$ *be a fitness function with extension to the domain* $\Delta^n \times \Delta^n$ *as in (2.6).*

a. *A pair* (μ, b), *where* $\mu \in \mathcal{P}(\mathcal{T})$ *and* $b = (b_T)_{T \in C(\mu)} \in B(\mu)$, *is stable w.r.t.* π *if the following conditions hold:*
   i. *For every* $T', T'' \in C(\mu)$ *we have* $\Pi_{T'}(\mu \mid b) = \Pi_{T''}(\mu \mid b)$.
   ii. *There exists an* $\epsilon' > 0$ *such that for every* $T \in \mathcal{T}$, $\epsilon \in (0, \epsilon')$, $T_\mu \in C(\mu)$ *and* $\bar{b} \in B((1 - \epsilon)\mu + \epsilon \, \delta_T \mid b)$ *we have*

$$\Pi_{T_\mu}((1 - \epsilon)\mu + \epsilon \, \delta_T \mid \bar{b}) \geq \Pi_T((1 - \epsilon)\mu + \epsilon \, \delta_T \mid \bar{b}), \qquad (2.8)$$

   where $B((1 - \epsilon)\mu + \epsilon \, \delta_T \mid b) \equiv \{ \tilde{b} \in B((1 - \epsilon)\mu + \epsilon \, \delta_T) :$ *For every* $T' \in C(\mu)$ *we have* $\tilde{b}_{T' \mid C(\mu)} = b_{T'} \}$.
b. *A population* $\mu \in P(\mathcal{T})$ *is stable w.r.t.* π *if there exists an equilibrium configuration* $b = (b_T)_{T \in C(\mu)} \in B(\mu)$ *such that the pair* (μ, b) *is stable w.r.t.* π.
c. *A strategy* $\sigma_s \in \Delta^n$ *is stable w.r.t.* π *if there exists a pair* (μ, b) *which is stable w.r.t.* π *and where for any* $T \in C(\mu)$ *we have* $b_T = \sigma_s$.

Parts *a.* and *b.* in Definition 2.19 are slightly modified versions of the stability concept proposed in [14]. We add a new stability definition for strategies in part *c.* In principle, a strategy satisfying the latter condition could be called an 'indirect evolutionary stable strategy'. Remember that in standard evolutionary game theory a strategy is evolutionary stable (cf. [37]) if with every other strategy, while played with sufficient low frequency in the mixed population, a strictly lower average fitness is obtained. For the current model the stability concept is yet more complex since preferences are formed indirectly via the success of the behavior they induce. Note that in Definition 2.19 we do not require strict inequality. A mutant-type agent may do as well as the incumbent-type agents, similar to the concept of a 'neutrally stable strategy' ([36]). This assumption seems reasonable because under a lot of equilibrium configurations several preference relations may imply equivalent behavior.

The stability concept in Definition 2.19 is static. We do not explicitly consider dynamic evolutionary processes that lead to a stable population of types. We rather investigate whether a particular population, once reached, is robust to threats posed by mutants. An explicit analysis of evolutionary dynamics with respect to preferences is carried out in [25]. Yet, the fitness values in that work and the set of admitted preferences are subject to a number of technical restrictions.

It turns out that a very useful concept for the characterization of stable populations is 'efficiency'. In the context of evolution of preferences it has been proposed in [14]. A strategy in Δ^n is called efficient if no other strategy yields a higher expected fitness when played against itself. That is, the strategy profile in which both players choose the efficient strategy is best in terms of the resulting fitness value among all symmetric strategy profiles. Obviously, an efficient strategy may not be unique. Moreover, it only depends on the fitness function, but not on the population. The formal definition is as follows.

Definition 2.20. *Let* $\pi : \bar{A} \times \bar{A} \to \mathbb{R}$ *be a fitness function with extension to the domain* $\Delta^n \times \Delta^n$ *as in (2.6). A strategy* $\sigma^* \in \Delta^n$ *is called efficient w.r.t.* π *if for any* $\sigma \in \Delta^n$ *we have*

$$\pi(\sigma^*, \sigma^*) \geq \pi(\sigma, \sigma). \tag{2.9}$$

Note that an efficient strategy always exists. This is due to the fact that the strategy set Δ^n is compact and that the fitness function extended to $\Delta^n \times \Delta^n$ is continuous (in particular, $\sigma \mapsto \pi(\sigma, \sigma)$ is a continuous map). In the following, such an efficient strategy will be denoted by σ^*, suppressing the particular fitness function with respect to which it is efficient. We call $\pi^* \equiv \pi(\sigma^*, \sigma^*)$ the efficient fitness. Of course, π^* is uniquely determined.

Our first result shows the robustness of a finding in [14] in our model with general, possibly non-expected utility preferences.

Proposition 2.21. *Let* $\pi : \bar{A} \times \bar{A} \to \mathbb{R}$ *be a fitness function with extension to the domain* $\Delta^n \times \Delta^n$ *as in (2.6). Suppose that the pair* (μ, b) *is stable w.r.t.* π. *Then, for any* $T, T' \in C(\mu)$ *we have*

$$\Pi_T(\mu \mid b) = \pi(b_T(T'), b_{T'}(T)) = \pi^*. \tag{2.10}$$

Proof. See Appendix A. $\square$

The main structure of the proof is similar to the one in the proof of Proposition 2 in [14]. However, as remarked earlier in the text, in our model a type is a preference relation on strategy profiles whereas in the cited work it is a utility function on the set of these profiles. Thus, in their model there are infinitely many different types which represent the same preference relation. Due to the fact that any population consists of only finitely many different types, this in particular implies that any preference relation satisfying the axioms in [14] is available as a potential entrant, independently of whether it is already part of the respective population or not. In our opinion, this modeling does not seem to be appropriate. By contrast, in our current model a preference relation is represented and characterized by a single type. A couple of technical additives become necessary in order to preserve the result.

Proposition 2.21 shows that given a stable pair (μ, b) all agents in the population must receive the same expected fitness from any match with any agent of any other type. Moreover, this fitness value must be equal to the efficient fitness. The argument behind this result is related to the 'secret handshake' ([49]). Suppose that the types in a stable population generate a fitness lower than π^* in every match. Then, by choosing an appropriate preference relation, we could find an entrant where the agents imitate an arbitrary incumbent-type agent in all matches with incumbent agents and correlates to the Nash equilibrium (σ^*, σ^*), where σ^* is an efficient strategy, when matched with another entrant-type agent. This entrant-type agent would outperform the incumbent-type agents in terms of average fitness and this preference relation could hence successfully invade the population. This contradicts stability.

Note that a Nash equilibrium of the material game, i.e. the game in which the players maximize their expected fitness, can be played within a stable population only if its associated fitness equals the efficient fitness π^*. In line with other findings about the evolution of preferences with full observability but contrary to most results in evolutionary game theory, evolution need not result in an aggregate play that resembles a Nash equilibrium of the material game. For detailed surveys of a number of these works see [65] and [35]. For instance, neither the non-Pareto optimal equilibrium in a coordination game nor the Nash equilibrium (in which both players do not cooperate) in a prisoner's dilemma game may ever be played within a stable population. Such examples will be discussed in Chap. 3.

As aforementioned, the result in Proposition 2.21 illustrates the robustness of our model with respect to the efficiency implications of stability as shown in [14]. The intuition is that with our richer type space there are more types that could possibly invade the population. Hence, stability is now even a stronger requirement as the conditions in Definition 2.19 have to hold against more potential entrants. Therefore, the average fitness which every type needs to generate in a stable population cannot be lower than with fewer potential entrants. It will be more interesting to see what we can say about sufficient conditions for stability. As we will see shortly, the results change substantially here. In particular, we obtain essential advancements with respect to existence issues.

2.5 A General Existence Result for Stable Populations

We are now in the position to present the main result of this chapter. It states that given any strategic preform with strategy sets Δ^n, where n is any finite number, and any fitness function, a stable population always exists.

This existence result is a conclusion of the following theorem. We show that for any efficient strategy we can find a stable population where the agents of all types from the support play this strategy in all their matches. Sloppily speaking, any efficient strategy is indirectly evolutionary stable.

Theorem 2.22. *Let $\pi : \bar{A} \times \bar{A} \to \mathbb{R}$ be a fitness function with extension to the domain $\Delta^n \times \Delta^n$ as in (2.6). If $\sigma^* \in \Delta^n$ is efficient w.r.t. π, then σ^* is stable w.r.t. π.*

Proof. See Appendix A. □

As we have seen in the previous section, an efficient strategy exists for any fitness function. Hence, the promised result is an immediate consequence of Theorem 2.22.

Corollary 2.23. *For any fitness function $\pi : \bar{A} \times \bar{A} \to \mathbb{R}$ with extension to the domain $\Delta^n \times \Delta^n$ as in (2.6) there exists a population $\mu \in \mathcal{P}(\mathcal{T})$ which is stable w.r.t. π.*

This finding is an important advantage over previous works on the evolution of preferences with full observability as well as many models in standard evolutionary game theory. In Dekel et al.'s model with expected utility maximizing agents ([14]) a stable population does not even exist in most 2×2 games. More precisely, for cases in which $\bar{A}$ contains exactly two elements and the strategy sets equal Δ^2, a stable population cannot be obtained as long as the (generic) fitness function is such that no pure strategy is efficient. No statement at all is made in [14] in this regard for three or more pure strategies. In contrast, we obtain existence for any finite number of pure strategies. In standard evolutionary game theory models in which a population is a distribution over the set of pure strategies, existence of a stable outcome is usually not secured either. For instance, an evolutionary stable strategy (ESS; [37]) does not necessarily exist. Our result is also an advancement compared to works in which evolutionary selection processes are explicitly modeled. For, such processes might easily diverge. For example, the predominant variant, Taylor and Jonker's replicator dynamics ([60]), may fail to converge when $n \geq 3$.

3

Examples: Properties of the Model

In the previous chapter we have seen that a stable population exists for any fitness function on the set of strategy profiles. Moreover, all agents of types in the support of such a stable population need to obtain the efficient fitness in each of their matches. In this chapter we like to illustrate the significance of the results and discuss differences to findings in other works on evolutionary issues with a couple of examples. In Sect. 3.1 we provide some statements about cooperative and non-cooperative behavior for the case in which the material game is a prisoner's dilemma. A pure coordination game is analyzed in Sect. 3.2. Finally, in Sect. 3.3 we discuss the model's potential to incorporate preferences that correspond to specific alternatives to von Neumann and Morgenstern's expected utility theory ([39]). Our particular focus here is on the important class of rank-dependent expected utility (RDEU) theories.

3.1 The 'Classic' Prisoner's Dilemma

First, we look at a case in which the fitness values correspond to the payoffs of a version of the classical prisoner's dilemma.

Example 3.1. Consider a two-player strategic preform with two pure strategies, i.e. with $\bar{A} = \{A, B\}$, and let the fitness values be as in Table 3.1. The strategy sets of the two players are given by Δ^2, the set of probability distributions on $\{A, B\}$. The fitness values for mixed strategy profiles in $\Delta^2 \times \Delta^2$ can be computed according to (2.6).

Table 3.1. Fitness values in a prisoner's dilemma

	A	B
A	3,3	0,10
B	10,0	1,1

In this example the pure strategy A ('Cooperation') is strictly dominated in terms of the fitness values by B ('Defection'). By considering

$$\max_{\sigma \in \Delta^2} 3\,(\sigma^1)^2 + 10\,\sigma^1\sigma^2 + 1\,(\sigma^2)^2 \tag{3.1}$$

and straightforward calculation one finds that the unique efficient strategy with respect to these fitness values is $\sigma^* = (\frac{2}{3}, \frac{1}{3})$. The associated fitness is $\pi^* \equiv \pi(\sigma^*, \sigma^*) = 3\frac{2}{3}$. Apparently, this value is strictly greater than 3, the fitness obtained through bilateral cooperation. This is naturally true since the pure strategy A, cooperation, is not efficient. From Proposition 2.21 we know that stability of a population requires every concerned agent, no matter of which type, to obtain the efficient fitness π^* in every match. Hence, in the current prisoner's dilemma neither a population in which agents always cooperate nor one with persistantly defecting players can ever be stable. Note that this may also be true in a model with only expected utility types. However, in such a setup a stable population with respect to the fitness values of Example 3.1 does not exist at all ([14], Proposition 3b). In Corollary 2.23 we have proven existence in our more general model. Stability is obtained, for instance, for a monomorphic population where agents always choose B if their opponent is not playing the efficient strategy σ^* and whose best responses to σ^* is the set

$$\left\{\lambda\,(1,0) + (1-\lambda)\,(0,1) \mid \lambda \in \left[0, \frac{2}{3}\right]\right\}, \tag{3.2}$$

alternatively for a monomorphic population in which the best-response correspondence induced by the only type is the identity function. In the associated equilibrium configuration the agents choose σ^* in all matches (and in doing so they receive a fitness of π^*). Note that there is just one type in this population. Hence, any agent is always matched with another agent of identical type. We abstain from providing a detailed description of a preference relation satisfying our continuity and convexity assumptions which induces this choice behavior. We rather refer to the proof of Theorem 2.22 and the results and proofs in Chap. 5.

The results here are in contrast to most findings in evolutionary game theory using explicit dynamic approaches according to which evolutionary forces select against pure strategies which are strictly dominated (or even iteratively strictly dominated) in terms of the fitness values. Examples are [1], [26] and [65]. One of the few exceptions is [15] which shows that a strictly dominated strategy (in terms of the fitness values) may not become extinct under some modified form of Taylor and Jonker's replicator dynamics ([60]).

Eventually, it is of course important to note that non-stability of cooperative behavior in Example 3.1 is due to this specific selection of the fitness values. If the fitness of 3 for the strategy profile (A, A) was replaced by 6, then this profile would be efficient. Hence, stability of a population would require (A, A) to be played in all matches. Note that this does not mean that cooperation would have to be a dominant strategy for agents whose type is in such a stable population. Rather, agents with such preferences are easily outperformed by a mutant agents who defect against opponents of this type and cooperate when matched with agents of its own type.

3.2 Coordination Games

In our second example we consider a situation in which the material game is a pure coordination game. The fitness values are 'doubly symmetric' in such a manner that for every $a_i, a_j \in \bar{A}$ we have $\pi(a_i, a_j) = \pi(a_j, a_i)$.

Example 3.2. Consider a two-player strategic preform with two pure strategies, i.e. with $\bar{A} = \{A, B\}$, and let the fitness values be as in Table 3.2.

Table 3.2. Fitness values in a coordination game

	A	B
A	10,10	0,0
B	0,0	1,1

The strategy sets of the two players are given by Δ^2, the set of probability distributions on $\{A, B\}$. The fitness values for mixed strategy profiles in $\Delta^2 \times \Delta^2$ can be computed according to (2.6).

This material game, i.e. the strategic game in which the preferences of the two players are represented by the fitness function, has two pure Nash equilibria, the strategy profiles (A, A) and (B, B). Obviously, the unique efficient strategy is A. Moreover, (A, A) is the only strategy profile which yields the efficient fitness of 10. Proposition 2.21 implies that given a stable population with respect to these fitness values A must be played in every match. This means that with the stability concept applied in this work, evolution particularly selects against the inefficient (or 'bad') equilibrium in coordination games. As discussed in Sect. 2.4, this urge towards efficiency is not a novel and exclusive conclusion from this model. Yet, there is a crucial and welcome difference to the well-known solution concepts from evolutionary game theory. For instance, the strategy profile (B, B) is an evolutionary stable strategy (ESS) for the fitness values of Example 3.2, and under the continuous replicator dynamics a population may converge to the inefficient equilibrium strategy B (cf. [32]). In the current model full observability of the opponents' preferences requires 'efficient play'. We refer to the discussion following Proposition 2.21 concerning this matter.

3.3 Rank-Dependent Expected Utility Theory

The type space that we have chosen in our model is very general and permits a wide range of preferences to occur in a population. In particular, preferences are no longer restricted to satisfy the von Neumann-Morgenstern assumptions. Non-expected utility maximizing behavior is explicitly embedded. However, in Definition 2.14 we require the preference relations in our type space to be continuous and to satisfy convexity on the set of own strategies. The latter assumption is crucial since, and despite its relative generality, it still excludes some sorts of preferences that have been studied in alternative models replacing von Neumann and Morgenstern's expected utility theory ([39]). In order to illustrate this issue, we consider the class of rank-dependent expected utility (RDEU) preferences. RDEU models have been first introduced in [45]. Axiomatizations are provided in [63] and [67], in the latter work with the utility function on the set of consequences being the identity function. To simplify matters, we restrict the treatment to cases in which the utility function on pure strategy profiles coincides with the fitness function. Preferences diverge from fitness maximization only in the mixed extension. On the set of pure strategy profiles they are indeed represented by the fitness function. That is to say, the preference relations that we consider here are assumed to satisfy the conditions of Yaari's dual theory of choice under risk ([67]). Formally, a preference relation $\succsim_Y$ on the set of strategy profiles of a strategic preform $(N, (\Delta^n, \Delta^n))$ can be represented $f : [0, 1] \to [0, 1]$ with

$$f(0) = 0 \text{ and } f(1) = 1 \tag{3.3}$$

such that for any $(\sigma_Y, \sigma_{-Y}), (\sigma'_Y, \sigma'_{-Y}) \in \Delta^n \times \Delta^n$ we have

$$(\sigma_Y, \sigma_{-Y}) \succsim_Y (\sigma'_Y, \sigma'_{-Y})$$

$$\iff \sum_{i=1}^{n^2} \pi(\bar{a}_i) \left[f\left(\sum_{j=i}^{n^2} p_j \right) - f\left(\sum_{j=i+1}^{n^2} p_j \right) \right]$$

$$\geq \sum_{i=1}^{n^2} \pi(\bar{a}_i) \left[f\left(\sum_{j=i}^{n^2} p'_j \right) - f\left(\sum_{j=i+1}^{n^2} p'_j \right) \right] \tag{3.4}$$

where $\bar{a}_i = (a_k, a_l)$ for some $k, l \in \{1, ..., n\}$ (and $\bar{a}_i \neq \bar{a}_{i'}$ for $i \neq i'$) such that

$$\pi(\bar{a}_1) \leq \ ... \ \leq \pi(\bar{a}_{n^2}) \tag{3.5}$$

and

$$p_i = \sigma_Y^k \sigma_{-Y}^l \tag{3.6}$$

for the specified k and l. The $\bar{a}_i$s are an increasing ordering of the pure strategy profiles in terms of the resulting fitness values. An agent with such preferences is maximizing her rank-dependent expected fitness.

In addition, we consider a fitness function which is such that no two pure strategy profiles induce the same fitness value (a so-called 'generic' fitness function). If the preference relations of two RDEU agents are represented by strictly convex fs, then the resulting two-player strategic game can have pure strategy Nash equilibria only ([46]).

Example 3.3. Consider a two-player strategic preform with two pure strategies, i.e. with $\bar{A} = \{A, B\}$, and let the fitness values be as in Table 3.3.

Table 3.3. Fitness values in Example 3.3

	A	B
A	1,1	10,20
B	20,10	0,0

The strategy sets of the two players are given by Δ^2, the set of probability distributions on $\{A, B\}$. The fitness values for mixed strategy profiles in $\Delta^2 \times \Delta^2$ can be computed according to (2.6).

We examine the case when two agents of an identical type T^{co} are matched. Thus, they have identical preferences represented in RDEU form. Let us assume that the probability transformation function is convex. The resulting game according to their preferences has exactly two Nash equilibria, (A, B) and (B, A). However, it has no symmetric Nash equilibrium. That is, for no $\sigma_{T^{co}} \in \Delta^n$ the profile $(\sigma_{T^{co}}, \sigma_{T^{co}})$ is a Nash equilibrium of that game. Therefore, the two agents cannot behave identically as we have required in Sect. 2.3. The reason for nonexistence of a mixed strategy Nash equilibrium is that the players are not willing to randomize among equally preferred pure strategies. The image sets of their best-response correspondences are not convex-valued and the requirements of Kakutani's fixed point theorem are therefore not fulfilled. Such a preference relation lies outside our type space $\mathcal{T}$.

Note that the case of convex probability transformation functions corresponds to a situation in which the decision-makers are risk averse, in any sense of the world. For the argument we refer to [67] and [50]. Also, a strong form of risk aversion for RDEU decision makers has been analyzed in [8]. A survey and discussion of these results, with special focus on dual theory preferences, is contained in [66].

It can be shown that existence of the appropriate Nash equilibria can be guaranteed only for RDEU types with (weakly) concave probability transformation functions. We omit the details. However, it is important to note that with concave transformation functions none of the agents can actually be risk averse. A setup with possibly risk-averse agents would probably be the more interesting and realistic case. If aiming at embedding agents with such preferences, one could weaken the premise that the outcome of a match is necessarily a Nash equilibrium. Alternatively, the assumption that the players cannot condition their choices on the positions in the game could be relaxed. We will not tackle these questions here.

4

Evolutionary Extinction of Expected Utility Preferences

Many papers in the past have focused on providing an evolutionary rationale for the expected utility theorem. Examples are the models in [29], [10] and [48]. An excellent survey of these works can be found in [49]. However, these authors assume that preferences derived originally from decision-theoretic problems. Typical objectives are the maximization of the probability of survival to the end, i.e. self-preservation, in a multi-period model or the expected number of offspring. In these models there is just a single decision-maker. Interactions with other agents are not involved. In this work we model evolution in strategic situations on the basis of the 'indirect evolutionary approach', where preferences govern the own behavior as well as the behavior of the opponents. It turns out that preferences which admit an expected utility representation may be unfavorable in such an environment. More precisely, we show that for 2×2 games in which the generic fitness values are such that no pure strategy is efficient, no type that has an expected utility representation may be an element of the support of a stable population. Evolution thus selects against expected utility maximization in this case. Neither can a monomorphic population of expected utility maximizers be stable nor can such agents co-exist along with agents that have other preferences. Expected utility preferences may of course survive in all situations in which a pure strategy is efficient. But even then agents with non-expected utility preferences still need not become extinct.

The chapter is structured as follows: In Sect. 4.1 we briefly introduce some simplifying terminology for the case of two pure strategies. Also, the main result about the failure of expected utility maximization in matters of stability is stated. In Sect. 4.2 we give an explicit characterization of those preference relations, i.e. the types, which can potentially be part of a stable population when expected utility preferences are selected against. Sect. 4.3 illustrates the idea behind our findings by means of an example. The proofs are again contained in the Appendix.

4.1 A Disfavor Result for Expected Utility Preferences

We stick to the model introduced in Chap. 2, but restrict our attention to 2×2 games. Formally, we consider strategic preforms with $n = 2$ pure strategies which are denoted by A and B in the following. The strategy sets of any two players are then given by Δ^2, the set of probability distributions on $\{A, B\}$. A fitness function is now defined on $\{A, B\} \times \{A, B\}$ and can be extended to the mixed strategy profiles in $\Delta^2 \times \Delta^2$ by taking expected values as in (2.6).

Note that we use the conventional terminology $n \times n$ game (or strategic preform) here to denote a two-player strategic game (or strategic preform) in which the strategy sets are Δ^n. Table 4.1 shows the fitness values given a 2×2 strategic preform with the two pure strategies A and B.

Table 4.1. Fitness values in 2×2 games

	A	B
A	a,a	b,c
B	c,b	d,d

Henceforth, we will assume that the fitness values are of this form, i.e. we have $a \equiv \pi(A, A)$, $b \equiv \pi(A, B)$, $c \equiv \pi(B, A)$ and $d \equiv \pi(B, B)$. Without loss of generality we can further suppose that $a \geq d$ holds. Otherwise, one could just rename the pure strategies A and B.

Within the range of 2×2 games, it turns out to be useful to simplify some notation. First of all, we identify a mixed strategy in Δ^2 with an element of the unit interval. For, such a $\sigma \in [0, 1]$ (or equivalently, $\sigma \in \Delta$) uniquely characterizes the strategy $(\sigma, 1 - \sigma) \in \Delta^2$. In the same manner, the equilibrium configuration accompanying a population μ of types will now be used as a family $(b_T)_{T \in C(\mu)}$ of functions $b_T : C(\mu) \to [0, 1]$, $T \in C(\mu)$, such that for any $T', T'' \in C(\mu)$ the pair

$$(b_{T'}(T''), b_{T''}(T')) \in [0, 1] \times [0, 1] \tag{4.1}$$

stands for the strategy profile

$$((b_{T'}(T''), 1 - b_{T'}(T'')), (b_{T''}(T'), 1 - b_{T''}(T'))) \in \Delta^2 \times \Delta^2, \qquad (4.2)$$

the Nash equilibrium played in the matches between agents of types T' and T''.

In Corollary 2.23 we have shown that for any fitness function on the strategy profiles of an $n \times n$ strategic preform a stable pair (μ, b) consisting of a population μ and an equilibrium configuration $b \in B(\mu)$ exists. Our model therefore generalizes the work in [14] in which existence is obtained even in the 2×2 case if and only if A is an efficient strategy or if $b = c$ holds while not making any statement at all for $n > 2$. This limitation in Dekel et al.'s model is due to the assumption that the agents, which may have arbitrary preferences on the set of pure strategy profiles, maximize their expected utility in the mixed extension of the game. Allowing for a much broader class of possible preferences on the set of mixed strategy profiles to occur in the population, we have derived existence for all interactions with any finite number of pure strategies. The main result of this chapter shows that, in addition, in the 2×2 case expected utility maximizers cannot survive the course of evolution for generic fitness functions if no pure strategy is efficient. More formally, no type that has an expected utility representation can occur in the support of a stable population if A is not efficient unless b equals c. These are exactly the cases in which [14] does not have existence of a stable pair. Thus, the latter work already demonstrates that populations consisting solely of expected utility types can always be successfully invaded by mutants. We show that, above all, expected utility maximizers cannot co-exist along with other types. No population composed of expected and non-expected utility types can ever be stable if the fitness values are as described above. Note that this is not true in case that A is efficient or if b equals c as we will see in Chap. 5.

The formal result is as follows.

Theorem 4.1. *Let $\pi : \{A, B\} \times \{A, B\} \to \mathbb{R}$ be a fitness function with extension to the domain $[0, 1] \times [0, 1]$ as in (2.6). Suppose that A is not efficient w.r.t. π and that we have $b \neq c$. If a population μ is stable w.r.t. π, then $C(\mu)$ does not contain any type that has an expected utility representation.*

Proof. See Appendix B.   □

4.2 Potential Stable Populations

We have seen in Theorem 4.1 that in the case of 2×2 games a stable population cannot contain any expected utility type unless a pure strategy is efficient or b equals c. In the latter case the fitness function would be 'doubly symmetric' in the sense described in Sect. 3.2. However, we know from Corollary 2.23 that a stable population does nevertheless exist for these fitness values. It is thus naturally to wonder which sorts of preferences may actually occur in the support of such a stable population. As the proof of Theorem 4.1 reveals, the strategy profile (σ^*, σ^*) must necessarily be the Nash equilibrium that is played in all matches within the stable population. Here, σ^* denotes the efficient strategy which is unique due to the assumption that neither pure strategy is efficient. Hence, for all agents of any type in the stable population, σ^* must be a best response to itself.

It turns out that additional requirements on the set of potential stable populations can be explicitly stated. In the present case we obtain formal properties of this set. This is the content of the following theorem.

Theorem 4.2. *Let* $\pi : \{A, B\} \times \{A, B\} \to \mathbb{R}$ *be a fitness function with extension to the domain* $[0, 1] \times [0, 1]$ *as in (2.6). Suppose that A is not efficient w.r.t. π and that we have $b \neq c$. Then, if a population μ is stable w.r.t. π, then $C(\mu)$ solely contains types $T \in \mathcal{T}$ with best-response correspondences that satisfy $\sigma^* \in \beta_T(\sigma^*)$ and for which we have*

i. *if $b > c \geq \pi^*$:*

$$
\beta_T(\sigma) \subseteq
\begin{cases}
\left[0, \frac{\pi^* - d - \sigma(b-d)}{\sigma(a+d-b-c)+c-d}\right] & \text{if } 0 \leq \sigma \leq \frac{c-\pi^*}{c-a} \\
[0, 1] & \text{if } \frac{c-\pi^*}{c-a} < \sigma < \frac{\pi^*-d}{b-d} \\
[\sigma^*, 1] & \text{if } \sigma = \sigma^* \\
\left(\frac{\pi^* - d - \sigma(b-d)}{\sigma(a+d-b-c)+c-d}, 1\right] & \text{if } \frac{\pi^*-d}{b-d} \leq \sigma \leq 1, \sigma \neq \sigma^*
\end{cases}
, \quad (4.3)
$$

ii. *if $b > c$ and $c < \pi^*$:*

$$
\beta_T(\sigma) \subseteq
\begin{cases}
[0, 1] & \text{if } 0 \leq \sigma < \frac{\pi^*-d}{b-d} \\
[\sigma^*, 1] & \text{if } \sigma = \sigma^* \\
\left(\frac{\pi^* - d - \sigma(b-d)}{\sigma(a+d-b-c)+c-d}, 1\right] & \text{if } \frac{\pi^*-d}{b-d} \leq \sigma \leq 1, \sigma \neq \sigma^*
\end{cases}
, \quad (4.4)
$$

iii. if $c > b \geq \pi^*$:

$$
\beta_T(\sigma) \subseteq \begin{cases} \left[0, \frac{\pi^* - d - \sigma(b-d)}{\sigma(a+d-b-c)+c-d}\right) & \text{if } 0 \leq \sigma \leq \frac{c-\pi^*}{c-a}, \ \sigma \neq \sigma^* \\ [0, \sigma^*] & \text{if } \sigma = \sigma^* \\ [0, 1] & \text{if } \frac{c-\pi^*}{c-a} < \sigma < \frac{\pi^* - d}{b-d} \\ \left[\frac{\pi^* - d - \sigma(b-d)}{\sigma(a+d-b-c)+c-d}, 1\right] & \text{if } \frac{\pi^* - d}{b-d} \leq \sigma \leq 1 \end{cases}, \quad (4.5)
$$

iv. if $c > b$ and $b < \pi^*$:

$$
\beta_T(\sigma) \subseteq \begin{cases} \left[0, \frac{\pi^* - d - \sigma(b-d)}{\sigma(a+d-b-c)+c-d}\right) & \text{if } 0 \leq \sigma \leq \frac{c-\pi^*}{c-a}, \ \sigma \neq \sigma^* \\ [0, \sigma^*] & \text{if } \sigma = \sigma^* \\ [0, 1] & \text{if } \frac{c-\pi^*}{c-a} < \sigma \leq 1 \end{cases}. \quad (4.6)
$$

Proof. See Appendix B. □

4.3 An Anti-Coordination Game

In this section we like to illustrate the two results and the characteristics of their proofs with an example. Basically, it is a simplified alternative to Example 3.3 with the fitness values to the pure strategy profiles (A, A) and (B, B) now being identical. The material game that we use here is an anti-coordination game. It has some similarities with a hawk-dove game (also known as 'chicken' game) and likewise with a battle-of-sexes example. Yet, in the original meaning of the latter game both players want to coordinate on a pure strategy (with opposite interests about which particular strategy to coordinate on). Here, the aim of two fitness maximizing players would be to coordinate on the choice of a different pure strategy, respectively.

Example 4.3. Consider a two-player strategic preform with two pure strategies, i.e. with $\bar{A} = \{A, B\}$, and let the fitness values be as in Table 4.2.

Table 4.2. Fitness values in an anti-coordination game

	A	B
A	0,0	5,10
B	10,5	0,0

The strategy sets of the two players are given by Δ^2, the set of probability distributions on $\{A, B\}$. The fitness values for mixed strategy profiles in $\Delta^2 \times \Delta^2$ can be computed according to (2.6).

In the formal description of Example 4.3 we have used the terminology and notation from Chap. 2. However, in the following discussion we will stick to the identification of the strategies in Δ^2 with elements from the unit interval etc. that we have introduced at the beginning of this chapter.

It is easily recognized that $\sigma^* = \frac{1}{2}$ is the unique efficient strategy with respect to the fitness values of Example 4.3 yielding an expected fitness of $\pi^* = 3.75$. Due to the uniqueness of the efficient strategy we have that $(\frac{1}{2}, \frac{1}{2})$ is the only symmetric strategy profile that renders this fitness. Therefore, it must in particular be the Nash equilibrium played in the matches with two agents of the same type in a stable population (remember that all agents of each type behave identically and must therefore play a symmetric Nash equilibrium when meeting each other). Now suppose that there is a type in that population which has a utility representation in expected utility form and for which $\frac{1}{2}$ is a best response to $\frac{1}{2}$. Then, A and B must also be best responses to $\frac{1}{2}$ because an agent with such preferences randomizes between two pure strategies only if she is indifferent among them. Above all, the independence axiom implies that the agent is indifferent among all randomizations among the two pure strategies. Exactly this property allows a particular mutant type to enter and to yield a higher average fitness than the expected utility type: T_0 is defined as the type where agents with these preferences are indifferent among all strategy profiles, independently of the action taken by their opponent. If this type enters and in the Nash equilibrium between any such agent and an expected utility maximizer the agent mixes with $\frac{1}{2}$ while the expected utility maximizer plays the pure strategy A (we have just seen that for her A is a best response to $\frac{1}{2}$), then she receives an expected fitness of 5 from this match whereas the expected utility maximizer only obtains 2.5. The set of best responses of a T_0 agent is a superset of any incumbent's set of best responses for any strategy taken by an opponent. This implies that a T_0 agent can adapt to an arbitrary incumbent's behavior in all other matches and, consequently, she obtains the efficient fitness π^* each time (remember that the population is assumed to be stable). Her overall average fitness is higher than that of the expected utility maximizer, independently of T_0's post-entry population share. Hence, type T_0 can successfully invade the population. Therefore, we have a contradiction to the assumption that the population comprising the expected utility type is stable.

In the following, we will outline the properties which preference relations need to fulfill in order to possibly be part of a stable population. The exposition is essentially a version of the proof of Theorem 4.2 applied to the specific fitness values of Example 4.3. It is intended to illustrate the ideas behind that proof.

For a population to be stable no mutant-type agent may ever receive an expected fitness which is strictly higher than π^* from any match with any agent from that population. Otherwise, the mutant type T_0 could enter in a sufficiently small proportion with those agents obtaining a fitness strictly higher than π^* from the matches with agents of this particular other type. In all matches with other incumbents, if these exist, T_0 agents imitate the behavior of any other incumbent yielding a fitness of π^* (remember that the population is assumed to be stable). Hence, a T_0 agent's total average fitness is strictly higher than π^*. As T_0's population share is very small, the incumbent agents' fitness is necessarily less than the fitness of the T_0 agents (actually it is close to π^* because matches with agents of the mutant type are very rare). Any incumbent's set of best responses to a given mixed strategy must therefore not include any mixed strategy such that the opponent's expected fitness from the resulting strategy profile is strictly higher than π^*.

Formally, let μ be a stable population. For all $T \in C(\mu)$, $\bar{\sigma}_e \in \Delta$ and $\sigma_T \in \beta_T(\bar{\sigma}_e)$ we must have

$$3.75 = \pi^* \geq 5\,\bar{\sigma}_e\,(1 - \sigma_T) + 10\,(1 - \bar{\sigma}_e)\,\sigma_T$$
$$= \sigma_T\,(10 - 15\,\bar{\sigma}_e) + 5\,\bar{\sigma}_e. \tag{4.7}$$

This implies that a necessary condition for stability is

$$\beta_T(\sigma_e) \subseteq \begin{cases} \left[0, \min\left\{1, \frac{3.75 - 5\,\bar{\sigma}_e}{10 - 15\,\bar{\sigma}_e}\right\}\right] & \text{if } \sigma_e < \frac{2}{3} \\ [0,1] & \text{if } \sigma_e = \frac{2}{3} \\ \left[\max\left\{0, \frac{3.75 - 5\,\bar{\sigma}_e}{10 - 15\,\bar{\sigma}_e}\right\}, 1\right] & \text{if } \sigma_e > \frac{2}{3} \end{cases} \tag{4.8}$$

In order to further characterize the set of stable populations, we investigate the cases in which an entrant-type agent obtain an expected fitness of exactly π^* from a match with an incumbent agent. As one can see from (4.7) this happens exactly for strategy profiles $(\sigma_T, \sigma_e) \in \Delta \times \Delta$ with $\sigma_T = \frac{3.75 - 5\,\sigma_e}{10 - 15\,\sigma_e}$, $\sigma_e \neq \frac{2}{3}$. Equality in (4.7) can never occur when σ_e is equal to $\frac{2}{3}$ as this is not an efficient strategy.

The incumbent's expected fitness from the profile $(\sigma_T, \bar{\sigma}_e)$ is

$$\pi(\sigma_T, \bar{\sigma}_e) = 5\,\sigma_T\,(1 - \bar{\sigma}_e) + 10\,(1 - \sigma_T)\,\bar{\sigma}_e$$
$$= \sigma_T\,(5 - 15\,\bar{\sigma}_e) + 10\,\bar{\sigma}_e. \tag{4.9}$$

The function

$$x \mapsto \frac{3.75 - 5x}{10 - 15x}\,(5 - 15x) + 10x - 3.75, \tag{4.10}$$

defined for $x \in [0, 1] \setminus \{\frac{2}{3}\}$, has a double null at $x = \frac{1}{2}$, no other null, a strictly positive value at $x = 1$ and a strictly negative value at $x = 0$ (due to a vertical asymptote at $x = \frac{2}{3}$).

Consequently, whenever a mutant agent receives a fitness of exactly π^* from such a match, the incumbent's expected fitness is still at least as large as long as $\bar{\sigma}_e > \frac{2}{3}$ or $\bar{\sigma}_e = \sigma^* = \frac{1}{2}$ holds. However, if $\bar{\sigma}_e < \frac{2}{3}$ and $\bar{\sigma}_e \neq \frac{1}{2}$, then the mutant could successfully enter the population.

Note that $\min\{1, \frac{3.75 - 5\,\bar{\sigma}_e}{10 - 15\,\bar{\sigma}_e}\} = 1$ (for $\bar{\sigma}_e < \frac{2}{3}$) if and only if $0.625 \leq \bar{\sigma}_e < \frac{2}{3}$ and that $\max\{0, \frac{3.75 - 5\,\bar{\sigma}_e}{10 - 15\,\bar{\sigma}_e}\} = 0$ (for $\bar{\sigma}_e > \frac{2}{3}$) if and only if $\frac{2}{3} < \bar{\sigma}_e \leq 0.75$.

All in all, we have the following result.

Remark 4.4. Let the fitness function π be as in Example 4.3. Then, if a population μ is stable w.r.t. π, then $C(\mu)$ solely contains types $T \in \mathcal{T}$ with best-response correspondences that satisfy

$$0.5 = \sigma^* \in \beta_T(\sigma^*) = \beta_T(0.5) \tag{4.11}$$

and for which we have

$$\beta_T(\sigma) \subseteq \begin{cases} [0, \frac{3.75 - 5\sigma}{10 - 15\sigma}) & \text{if } \sigma \leq 0.625 \text{ and } \sigma \neq 0.5 \\ [0, \frac{1}{2}] & \text{if } \sigma = 0.5 \\ [0, 1] & \text{if } 0.625 < \sigma < 0.75 \\ [\frac{3.75 - 5\sigma}{10 - 15\sigma}, 1] & \text{if } \sigma \geq 0.75 \end{cases} \tag{4.12}$$

The sufficiency of the requirements in Remark 4.4 for stability does not follow immediately. It is not clear that every population with such best-response correspondences together with an equilibrium configuration in which all agents play the efficient strategy σ^* in all matches is a stable pair with respect to the given fitness function. The problem here is with the uniformity of the invasion barrier. It needs to hold for any potential entrant from the type space and any post-entry equilibrium configuration.

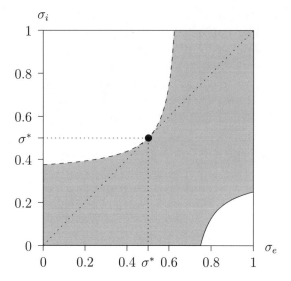

Fig. 4.1. The graphs of best-response correspondences induced by preferences in a stable population must lie inside the shaded area

We illustrate the set of preferences that may potentially occur in a stable population in Figure 4.1.

The shaded area indicates the pairs (σ_e, σ_i) such that σ_i may be a best response to σ_e. If the second component of a strategy profile outside this area is a best response to the first component, then such a preference relation can never be part of the support of a stable population. The diagonal line indicates the symmetric strategy profiles. Obviously, this line is completely comprised in the shaded area since the fitness values of these profiles are always at most π^*. Note that all preference relations in any stable population must be such that the efficient strategy is a best response to itself.

An interesting property of preference relations that induce best-response correspondences satisfying the requirements in Remark 4.4 is that they differ significantly from preferences represented by the fitness function. Neither is B allowed for as a best response to A nor can A be a best response to B for an agent of any type in a stable population. However, (A, B) and (B, A) are the two pure strategy Nash equilibria of the game in which both players maximize their expected fitness, i.e. the material game. The logic behind this observation is yet very intuitive. Suppose that a stable population contains a type such that the best response to A is B. Suppose further that a mutant, say type T_0, enters and in the post-entry population in the equilibrium of the matches of agents of these two types the T_0 agent plays A while the incumbent agent plays B. The entrance of T_0 requires that it is not already a member of the population, of course. This event is taken care of in all formal proofs, but we will omit it for our discussion here. Obviously, the incumbent agent receives an evolutionary fitness of 10 from these matches whereas the T_0 agent's fitness is only 5. However, 5 is still more than the efficient fitness of 3.75. Hence, if T_0 enters in sufficiently small proportion, then the incumbent's matches with T_0 agents are very rare and her average fitness is lower than the fitness of the entrant-type agent.

Note that when A is efficient with respect to the given fitness function or when b equals c, then some sorts of expected utility preferences can be part of stable populations, of course. This will become clear from the proofs of Lemmas 5.13, 5.14 and 5.16. An analysis of other preference relations in such stable populations appears less interesting then.

5

Evolution with More Sophisticated Types

The current evolutionary model allows for very general preferences to occur in the support of a population. In particular, non-expected utility maximizing behavior is explicitly embedded. As we have seen in Chap. 2, this broadness enables us to prove existence of a stable population for any finite number of pure strategies. An objection that could possibly be raised against this setup is that some very abstract and peculiar preferences could emerge. Although preferences need to satisfy specific continuity and convexity properties, they may happen to be quite arbitrary and need not be close the fitness values in any sense. It seems thus naturally to redo some of the analysis with a space of considerably higher developed agents. In this chapter we require preferences on strategy profiles to satisfy the betweenness axiom on the own strategy space. Betweenness has been proposed as a weaker alternative to the independence axiom of expected utility theory, mainly in order to obtain conformity with the choice behavior generating the well-known paradoxes of the latter theory, e.g. the common consequence effect and the common ratio effect ([2], [27]). Thus, by imposing betweenness we move a bit back in the direction of expected utility theory and create more structure on the type space. For, this type space now contains fewer elements since every preference relation satisfying betweenness in the first component is also convex in the first component. Yet, with this restricted set of possible preferences existence of a stable population can be maintained at least for the 2×2 case, i.e. with two pure strategies. Moreover, in this case we still obtain full equivalence between efficiency and stability of a strategy.

In Sect. 5.1 we state the definition of betweenness in the first component and analyze some implications. In particular, for any agent with preferences which satisfy betweenness the set of best responses to any given strategy of the opponent necessarily includes a pure strategy. Furthermore, we introduce the restricted type space. As in Chap. 2, stability of a population requires that all agents with preference relations from the support of this population receive the efficient fitness in all their matches. The existence and equivalence results are contained in Sect. 5.2.

5.1 The Restricted Type Space

We continue to work with the setup introduced in Chap. 2. In particular, we further on consider a two-player strategic preform $(N, (\Delta^n, \Delta^n))$, where n is some finite number. In the following definition the notion of betweenness on the own strategy space of a preference relation on $\Delta^n \times \Delta^n$ is introduced.

Definition 5.1. *A preference relation $\succsim_T$ on $\Delta^n \times \Delta^n$ satisfies betweenness in the first component if for any $\sigma_T, \sigma'_T, \sigma_{-T} \in \Delta^n$ such that $(\sigma_T, \sigma_{-T}) \succsim_T (\sigma'_T, \sigma_{-T})$ and for any $\alpha \in [0, 1]$ the preference patterns*

i. $(\sigma_T, \sigma_{-T}) \succsim_T (\alpha\, \sigma_T + (1 - \alpha)\, \sigma'_T,\ \sigma_{-T})$,
ii. $(\alpha\, \sigma_T + (1 - \alpha)\, \sigma'_T,\ \sigma_{-T}) \succsim_T (\sigma'_T, \sigma_{-T})$

hold.

Our version is slightly weaker than the predominantly used definition of betweenness in which all preference patterns are replaced by strict preferences. The terminology 'betweenness' derives from the axiom's original use within the analysis of choices among lotteries in a single decision-maker setup. Here, in terms of the preference relation of an agent any probabilistic mixture of two lotteries must lie 'between' the two lotteries. More formally, the decision-maker must prefer the better lottery over the mixture but needs to prefer the mixture over the weaker lottery. The application of betweenness in our game-theoretic context is very similar. The strategy profile $(\alpha\, \sigma_T + (1 - \alpha)\, \sigma'_T,\ \sigma_{-T})$ is a probabilistic mixture of the profiles (σ_T, σ_{-T}) and (σ'_T, σ_{-T}). Note that in order to work with Nash equilibria later we need to compare strategy profiles with identical strategy choices of the opponent only.

Obviously, every preference relation which has a representation in expected utility form, i.e. which fulfills a version of the independence axiom, also satisfies betweenness in the first component. For, note that in Definition 5.1 mixtures with any third strategy profile are not considered. In the next proposition we show that betweenness in the first component implies convexity in the first component. Therefore, all preference relations on $\Delta^n \times \Delta^n$ which are continuous and satisfy betweenness are necessarily elements of our type space $\mathcal{T}$ introduced in Chap. 2.

Proposition 5.2. *Let a preference relation* $\succsim_T$ *on* $\Delta^n \times \Delta^n$ *satisfy betweenness in the first component. Then,* $\succsim_T$ *is convex in the first component.*

Proof. Let $(\bar{\sigma}_T, \bar{\sigma}_{-T}) \in \Delta^n \times \Delta^n$ and suppose that $\sigma'_T, \sigma''_T \in \Delta^n$ are such that $(\sigma'_T, \bar{\sigma}_{-T}) \succsim_T (\bar{\sigma}_T, \bar{\sigma}_{-T})$ and $(\sigma''_T, \bar{\sigma}_{-T}) \succsim_T (\bar{\sigma}_T, \bar{\sigma}_{-T})$ hold. Let $\alpha \in [0, 1]$. We must show that $(\alpha\,\sigma'_T + (1 - \alpha)\,\sigma''_T,\ \bar{\sigma}_{-T}) \succsim_T (\bar{\sigma}_T, \bar{\sigma}_{-T})$.

By completeness of $\succsim_T$ we must have $(\sigma'_T, \bar{\sigma}_{-T}) \succsim_T (\sigma''_T, \bar{\sigma}_{-T})$ or vice versa. W.l.o.g. we may assume that the former holds true. As $\succsim_T$ satisfies betweenness in the first component, this yields

$$(\alpha\,\sigma'_T + (1 - \alpha)\,\sigma''_T,\ \bar{\sigma}_{-T}) \succsim_T (\sigma''_T, \bar{\sigma}_{-T}). \tag{5.1}$$

In addition, by assumption, we have $(\sigma''_T, \bar{\sigma}_{-T}) \succsim_T (\bar{\sigma}_T, \bar{\sigma}_{-T})$. Combined and by transitivity of $\succsim_T$, we obtain

$$(\alpha\,\sigma'_T + (1 - \alpha)\,\sigma''_T, \bar{\sigma}_{-T}) \succsim_T (\bar{\sigma}_T, \bar{\sigma}_{-T}) \tag{5.2}$$

which proves the claim.   □

For any strategy in Δ^n the support specifies the pure strategies in $\bar{A}$ which are assigned strictly positive probabilities, i.e. it contains the pure strategies among which the player mixes.

Definition 5.3. *The support of a strategy* $\sigma_T \in \Delta^n$*, denoted by* $\mathrm{supp}(\sigma_T)$*, is the set* $\{a_i \in \bar{A} \mid \sigma_T^i > 0\}$*.*

The following proposition shows that, given continuity and betweenness in the first component, whenever a mixed strategy σ_T is a best response to an opponent's action there must be at least one pure strategy in the support of σ_T which is an alternative best response. In particular, a pure-strategy best response always exists. Randomization can never be strictly preferred. This is in contrast to expected utility theory where a decision-maker must always be indifferent between choosing an 'optimal' mixed strategy or any pure strategy in its support.

Proposition 5.4. *Let a preference relation* $\succsim_T$ *on* $\Delta^n \times \Delta^n$ *satisfy betweenness in the first component and continuity. Suppose that* $(\bar{\sigma}_T, \bar{\sigma}_{-T}) \in \Delta^n \times \Delta^n$ *is such that* $\bar{\sigma}_T \in \beta_T(\bar{\sigma}_{-T})$ *holds. Then, there exists* $a_i \in \mathrm{supp}(\bar{\sigma}_T)$ *such that* $a_i \in \beta_T(\bar{\sigma}_{-T})$*. In particular,* $\beta_T(\bar{\sigma}_{-T})$ *contains a pure strategy.*

Proof. For the purpose of contradiction we assume that such an a_i does not exist, i.e. for any $a_k \in \text{supp}(\bar{\sigma}_T)$ we have $a_k \notin \beta_T(\bar{\sigma}_{-T})$. This implies that for any $a_k \in \text{supp}(\bar{\sigma}_T)$ the following preference pattern must hold:

$$(\bar{\sigma}_T, \bar{\sigma}_{-T}) \succ_T (a_k, \bar{\sigma}_{-T}). \tag{5.3}$$

Let $J \equiv |\text{supp}(\bar{\sigma}_T)|$, i.e. J is the cardinality of the support of $\bar{\sigma}_T$. W.l.o.g. we can assume that $\text{supp}(\bar{\sigma}_T) = \{a_1, ..., a_J\}$ and that we have

$$(a_1, \bar{\sigma}_{-T}) \succsim_T (a_2, \bar{\sigma}_{-T}), \ ... \ , (a_{J-1}, \bar{\sigma}_{-T}) \succsim_T (a_J, \bar{\sigma}_{-T}). \tag{5.4}$$

By the definition of betweenness in the first component,

$$(a_{J-1}, \bar{\sigma}_{-T}) \succsim_T (\alpha_{J-1}\, a_{J-1} + (1 - \alpha_{J-1})\, a_J, \ \bar{\sigma}_{-T}) \tag{5.5}$$

holds true for all $\alpha_{J-1} \in [0, 1]$. By repeated application of this argument we obtain that

$$\forall \, \alpha'_1, ..., \alpha'_J \in [0, 1] \ \text{s.t.} \ \sum_{j=1}^{J} \alpha'_j = 1 :$$
$$(a_1, \bar{\sigma}_{-T}) \succsim_T (\sum_{j=1}^{J} \alpha'_j \, a_j, \ \bar{\sigma}_{-T}). \tag{5.6}$$

However, for $\bar{\sigma}_T^1, ..., \bar{\sigma}_T^J$, which obviously satisfy $\sum_{j=1}^{J} \bar{\sigma}_T^j = 1$, we have that

$$(\bar{\sigma}_T, \bar{\sigma}_{-T}) = (\sum_{j=1}^{J} \bar{\sigma}_T^j \, a_j, \ \bar{\sigma}_{-T}). \tag{5.7}$$

For these coefficients the preference pattern in (5.6) contradicts the one in (5.3).

Due to the compactness of Δ^n and continuity of $\succsim_T$ we have that for any $\bar{\sigma}_{-T} \in \Delta^n$ the set $\beta_T(\bar{\sigma}_{-T})$ is non-empty. Thus, by the first part of the proof, it must contain a pure strategy. □

Having investigated an implication for preferences on strategy profiles with the betweenness property on the own strategy space, we now come back to our analysis of the evolution of preferences. We restrict the type space introduced in Sect. 2.2.2 to those preference relations that, in addition to continuity, satisfy betweenness. As we have seen in Proposition 5.2, this is a stronger requirement than convexity on the own strategy space.

Definition 5.5. *Let $(N, (\Delta^n, \Delta^n))$ be a two-player strategic preform. The restricted type space, denoted by $\mathcal{T_R}$, is the set of all preference relations on $\Delta^n \times \Delta^n$ which satisfy betweenness in the first component and are continuous.*

As $\mathcal{T_R}$ is a subset of $\mathcal{T}$, the following proposition about the existence of a Nash equilibrium is an immediate consequence of Proposition 2.16.

Proposition 5.6. *For any two types $T, T' \in \mathcal{T_R}$ the two-player strategic game $(N, (\Delta^n, \Delta^n), (\succsim_T, \succsim_{T'}))$ has a Nash equilibrium.*

Likewise, the next result follows directly from Proposition 2.18.

Proposition 5.7. *Let $T \in \mathcal{T_R}$. The two-player strategic game $(N, (\Delta^n, \Delta^n), (\succsim_T, \succsim_T))$ has a symmetric Nash equilibrium, i.e. there exists $\sigma_T^{SN} \in \Delta^n$ such that $(\sigma_T^{SN}, \sigma_T^{SN})$ is a Nash equilibrium.*

In the following we restate the familiar concepts from Chap. 2 adapted to the restricted type space of this chapter. Since there are no changes of the contents of these definitions, we pass on providing in-depth discussions. In lieu thereof, we refer to our exposition in Sects. 2.2, 2.3 and 2.4.

Definition 5.8. *Let $(N, (\Delta^n, \Delta^n))$ be a two-player strategic preform. A $\mathcal{T_R}$-population is a function $\mu_{\mathcal{R}} : \mathcal{T_R} \to [0, 1]$ such that the following conditions are satisfied:*

i. $C(\mu_{\mathcal{R}}) \equiv \{T \in \mathcal{T_R} \mid \mu_{\mathcal{R}}(T) > 0\}$ is finite,
ii. $\sum_{T \in C(\mu_{\mathcal{R}})} \mu_{\mathcal{R}}(T) = 1$.

The set of all $\mathcal{T_R}$-populations is denoted by $\mathcal{P}(\mathcal{T_R})$.

In the remainder of this chapter we will commonly omit the prefix referring to the restricted type space. This should not cause any confusion. In the very same way as above we deal with equilibrium configurations and stability.

Definition 5.9. *Let $\mu_{\mathcal{R}}$ be a $\mathcal{T_R}$-population with support $C(\mu_{\mathcal{R}})$. A family $(b_T)_{T \in C(\mu_{\mathcal{R}})}$ of functions $b_T : C(\mu_{\mathcal{R}}) \to \Delta^n$, $T \in C(\mu_{\mathcal{R}})$, is called a $\mathcal{T_R}$-equilibrium configuration if for any $T', T'' \in C(\mu_{\mathcal{R}})$ the strategy profile $(b_{T'}(T''), b_{T''}(T'))$ is a Nash equilibrium of the two-player strategic game $(N, (\Delta^n, \Delta^n), (\succsim_{T'}, \succsim_{T''}))$.*

We denote the set of all $\mathcal{T_R}$-equilibrium configurations given $\mu_{\mathcal{R}}$ by $B(\mu_{\mathcal{R}})$. Given a $\mathcal{T_R}$-population $\mu_{\mathcal{R}}$ and a $\mathcal{T_R}$-equilibrium configuration

$b = (b_T)_{T \in C(\mu_{\mathcal{R}})} \in B(\mu_{\mathcal{R}})$, we can compute the average fitness of agents of type T in $C(\mu_{\mathcal{R}})$:

$$\Pi_T(\mu_{\mathcal{R}} \mid b) \equiv \sum_{T' \in C(\mu_{\mathcal{R}})} \mu_{\mathcal{R}}(T') \, \pi(b_T(T'), b_{T'}(T)). \tag{5.8}$$

In the following definition of stability we have entirely dispensed with a type space indexing in order to keep the model and the intuition clear enough.

Definition 5.10. Let $\pi : \bar{A} \times \bar{A} \to \mathbb{R}$ be a fitness function with extension to the domain $\Delta^n \times \Delta^n$ as in (2.6).

a. A pair $(\mu_{\mathcal{R}}, b)$, where $\mu_{\mathcal{R}} \in P(\mathcal{T}_{\mathcal{R}})$ and $b = (b_T)_{T \in C(\mu_{\mathcal{R}})} \in B(\mu_{\mathcal{R}})$, is stable w.r.t. π if the following conditions hold:
    i.   For every $T', T'' \in C(\mu_{\mathcal{R}})$ we have $\Pi_{T'}(\mu_{\mathcal{R}} \mid b) = \Pi_{T''}(\mu_{\mathcal{R}} \mid b)$.
    ii. There exists an $\epsilon' > 0$ such that for every $T \in \mathcal{T}_{\mathcal{R}}$, $\epsilon \in (0, \epsilon')$, $T_{\mu_{\mathcal{R}}} \in C(\mu_{\mathcal{R}})$ and $\bar{b} \in B((1 - \epsilon)\mu_{\mathcal{R}} + \epsilon \, \delta_T \mid b)$ we have

$$\Pi_{T_{\mu_{\mathcal{R}}}}((1 - \epsilon)\mu_{\mathcal{R}} + \epsilon \, \delta_T \mid \bar{b}) \geq \Pi_T((1 - \epsilon)\mu_{\mathcal{R}} + \epsilon \, \delta_T \mid \bar{b}), \tag{5.9}$$

    where $B((1 - \epsilon)\mu_{\mathcal{R}} + \epsilon \, \delta_T \mid b) \equiv \{\tilde{b} \in B((1 - \epsilon)\mu_{\mathcal{R}} + \epsilon \, \delta_T) : \text{For every } T' \in C(\mu_{\mathcal{R}}) \text{ we have } \tilde{b}_{T' \mid C(\mu_{\mathcal{R}})} = b_{T'}\}$.
b. A $\mathcal{T}_{\mathcal{R}}$-population $\mu_{\mathcal{R}} \in P(\mathcal{T}_{\mathcal{R}})$ is stable w.r.t. π if there exists an equilibrium configuration $b = (b_T)_{T \in C(\mu_{\mathcal{R}})} \in B(\mu_{\mathcal{R}})$ such that the pair $(\mu_{\mathcal{R}}, b)$ is stable w.r.t. π.
c. A strategy $\sigma_s \in \Delta^n$ is stable w.r.t. π if there exists a pair $(\mu_{\mathcal{R}}, b)$ which is stable w.r.t. π and where for any $T \in C(\mu_{\mathcal{R}})$ we have $b_T = \sigma_s$.

Just as in the model of Chap. 2 as well as in Dekel et al.'s setup with expected utility types ([14]) we derive that in a stable population with types from the restricted type space $\mathcal{T}_{\mathcal{R}}$ all types must generate the efficient fitness for all agents in all matches.

Proposition 5.11. Let $\pi : \bar{A} \times \bar{A} \to \mathbb{R}$ be a fitness function with extension to the domain $\Delta^n \times \Delta^n$ as in (2.6). Suppose that the pair $(\mu_{\mathcal{R}}, b)$ is stable w.r.t. π. Then, for any $T, T' \in C(\mu_{\mathcal{R}})$ we have

$$\Pi_T(\mu_{\mathcal{R}} \mid b) = \pi(b_T(T'), b_{T'}(T)) = \pi^*. \tag{5.10}$$

Proof. See Appendix C. □

As discussed above, our type space $\mathcal{T}_\mathcal{R}$ is sort of an intermediate case between Dekel et al.'s treatment with expected utility maximizers ([14]) and the type space $\mathcal{T}$ used in Chap. 2 of this work where, besides from a standard continuity assumption, only a certain form of convexity is imposed on preferences. In the latter two models the efficient fitness in each match is a necessary condition for stability of a population. Hence, the result in Proposition 5.11 should not be surprising. Almost all arguments in its proof can be carried forward from the proof of Proposition 2.21.

At this point it thus seems more interesting to seek for sufficient conditions for stability. In Theorem 2.22 we have derived a very general result, yet with the downside of a type space that contains some fewer intuitive preference relations. Such a universal finding is not obtained with the restricted type space of the current chapter. However, the next theorem shows that if a pure strategy is efficient with respect to the given fitness function and if the profile in which both players choose this particular strategy is a strict Nash equilibrium of the material game, then the strategy is stable with respect to the fitness function.

Theorem 5.12. *Let $\pi : \bar{A} \times \bar{A} \to \mathbb{R}$ be a fitness function with extension to the domain $\Delta^n \times \Delta^n$ as in (2.6). If a pure strategy $a_i \in \bar{A}$ is efficient w.r.t. π and if $\pi(a_i, a_i) > \pi(a_j, a_i)$ holds for all pure strategies $a_j \in \bar{A} \setminus \{a_i\}$, then a_i is stable w.r.t. π.*

Proof. See Appendix C. $\qquad\qquad\qquad\qquad\qquad\qquad\qquad\qquad\qquad$ □

The statement in Theorem 5.12 is an analog to the one in Proposition 1 in [14]. However, and contrary to the latter work, we are again able to achieve significantly stronger results. Our main finding in Chap. 2, according to which efficiency of a strategy with respect to the fitness function necessarily implies its stability, proves to be sustainable for the case of two pure strategies, i.e. when $\bar{A}$ contains exactly two elements. The derivation of this conclusion is the topic of the next section.

5.2 Existence in the 2 × 2 Case

We stick again to the setup of Chap. 4 where the attention has been restricted to 2×2 games. Formally, we consider strategic preforms with two pure strategies which will be subsequently denoted by A and B. The strategy sets of any two players are then given by Δ^2, the set of probability distributions on $\{A, B\}$. A fitness function is now defined on $\{A, B\} \times \{A, B\}$ and can be extended to the mixed strategy profiles in $\Delta^2 \times \Delta^2$ by taking expected values as in (2.6).

The matrix in Table 5.1 shows the fitness values given a 2×2 strategic preform with the two pure strategies A and B.

Table 5.1. Fitness values in the 2×2 case

	A	B
A	a,a	b,c
B	c,b	d,d

Remember that w.l.o.g. we can assume as in Chap. 4 that $a \geq d$ holds. Also, in all proofs of this section we will again identify a strategy $\sigma = (\sigma^1, \sigma^2) \in \Delta^2$ with the element $\sigma^1 \in [0, 1]$ (also denoted $\sigma^1 \in \Delta$). Equilibrium configurations and Nash equilibria are used accordingly. However, all results are formulated with strategies in Δ^2.

In order to coherently structure our arguments, we will develop the main existence result of this chapter in a succession of lemmas. The first of those is the only statement in this section which also holds true in a setup with exclusively expected utility maximizers ([14], Proposition 3a).

Lemma 5.13. *Let* $\pi : \bar{A} \times \bar{A} \to \mathbb{R}$ *be a fitness function with extension to the domain* $\Delta^2 \times \Delta^2$ *as in (2.6). If A is efficient w.r.t. π, then A is stable w.r.t. π.*

Proof. See Appendix C. $\square$

If, in addition to the pure strategy A, some other strategy $\sigma^* \neq A$ is efficient, then we must necessarily have $\pi(\sigma^*, \sigma^*) = \pi(A, A) = \pi^* = a$. We show in the next lemma that in this case the strategy σ^* is also stable with respect to π.

Lemma 5.14. *Let* $\pi : \bar{A} \times \bar{A} \to \mathbb{R}$ *be a fitness function with extension to the domain* $\Delta^2 \times \Delta^2$ *as in (2.6). Suppose that A is efficient w.r.t. π. If $\sigma^* \in \Delta^2$ is efficient w.r.t. π, then σ^* is stable w.r.t. π.*

Proof. See Appendix C. $\square$

The issue of the potential stability of an efficient mixed strategy conditional on the co-existence of the efficient pure strategy A is not investigated in Proposition 3 in [14]. The authors' analysis of stability implications for any efficient mixed strategy applies only to the case in which the two pure strategies are not efficient. We show in the next example that in Dekel et al.'s setting an efficient mixed strategy need not be stable with respect to the fitness function given that A is efficient.

Example 5.15. Consider a two-player strategic preform with two pure strategies, i.e. with $\bar{A} = \{A, B\}$, and let the fitness values be as in Table 5.2.

Table 5.2. Fitness values in Example 5.15

	A	B
A	1,1	0,2
B	2,0	1,1

The strategy sets of the two players are given by Δ^2, the set of probability distributions on $\{A, B\}$. The fitness values for mixed strategy profiles in $\Delta^2 \times \Delta^2$ can be computed according to (2.6).

For the fitness values in Example 5.15 and by (2.6), we have for any $\sigma \in [0, 1]$ that

$$\pi(\sigma, \sigma) = \sigma^2 + (1 - \sigma)^2 + 2\,\sigma(1 - \sigma) = 1 \qquad (5.11)$$

holds. Therefore, all strategies in $[0, 1]$ are efficient w.r.t. π. Let $\sigma' \in (0, 1)$ and suppose that σ' is stable w.r.t. π. For any type T_{EU} with an expected utility representation in a corresponding stable population $\mu_{\mathcal{R}}$ such that σ' is played in all matches, the best-response correspondence $\beta_{T_{EU}}$ must satisfy $\beta_{T_{EU}}(\sigma') = [0, 1]$. Consider an entrant T_e generating a best-response correspondence $\beta_{T_e} : [0, 1] \Rightarrow [0, 1]$ as follows:

$$\beta_{T_e}(\sigma) = \begin{cases} [0, 1] & \text{if } \sigma = 1 \\ \{1\} & \text{otherwise} \end{cases} . \qquad (5.12)$$

This best-response correspondence may come from expected utility preferences. Take, for instance, a preference relation $\succsim_{T_e}$ which is represented by the utility function $u_{T_e} : [0, 1] \times [0, 1] \to \mathbb{R}$ defined by

$$u_{T_e}(\sigma_T, \sigma_{-T}) = \sigma_T\,(1 - \sigma_{-T}). \qquad (5.13)$$

The function u_{T_e} has an expected utility form with a von Neumann-Morgenstern utility function $u_{VNM} : \{A, B\} \times \{A, B\} \to \mathbb{R}$ such that

$$u_{VNM}(A, B) = 1,$$
$$u_{VNM}(A, A) = u_{VNM}(B, A) = u_{VNM}(B, B) = 0. \tag{5.14}$$

Hence, T_e is in Dekel et al.'s type space. Suppose that in the post-entry equilibrium configuration $\bar{b}$ the equilibrium which is played when an agent of the entrant type and an incumbent of type T_{EU} are matched is $(\sigma_e, \sigma_i) \equiv (\bar{b}_{T_e}(T_{EU}), \bar{b}_{T_{EU}}(T_e)) = (\sigma', 1)$. The entrant-type agent's expected fitness from these matches is

$$\sigma' + 2(1 - \sigma') > 1 = \pi^*. \tag{5.15}$$

The average fitness generated by the incumbent and the entrant are, respectively, given by

$$\Pi_{T_{EU}}((1 - \epsilon)\,\mu_{\mathcal{R}} + \epsilon\,\delta_{T_e} \mid \bar{b}) = (1 - \epsilon) + \epsilon\,\sigma' < 1. \tag{5.16}$$

and

$$\Pi_{T_e}((1 - \epsilon)\,\mu_{\mathcal{R}} + \epsilon\,\delta_{T_e} \mid \bar{b})$$
$$= (1 - \epsilon)(\sigma' + 2(1 - \sigma')) + \epsilon > 1. \tag{5.17}$$

Hence, if entering in any strictly positive proportion, the entrant agent can successfully outperform the T_{EU} agents. This contradicts the assumption that T_{EU} is an element of the stable population $\mu_{\mathcal{R}}$. Since in [14] all agents have an expected utility representation, the entrant T_e would generate a strictly higher average fitness than every incumbent in $C(\mu_{\mathcal{R}})$.

Note that theses arguments for non-stability can be brought forward to all cases of co-existence of efficient mixed and efficient pure strategies unless the fitness function π is such that $a = b = c = d$ holds. In contrast to Dekel et al.'s model with expected utility types ([14]), the stability implication can generally be carried over to all efficient mixed strategies in the setup of this chapter with preferences that satisfy betweenness in the first component. The co-efficiency of the pure strategy A is not required as we show in the following lemma.

Lemma 5.16. *Let* $\pi : \bar{A} \times \bar{A} \to \mathbb{R}$ *be a fitness function with extension to the domain* $\Delta^2 \times \Delta^2$ *as in (2.6). Suppose that A is not efficient w.r.t. π. Then, if $\sigma^* \in \Delta^2$ is efficient w.r.t. π, the strategy σ^* is stable w.r.t. π.*

Proof. See Appendix C. □

Combining Lemmas 5.13, 5.14 and 5.16 we have the following result. Any efficient strategy is stable with respect to the given fitness function. We can therefore always find a stable population where all agents of types from the support play that particular strategy in all their matches.

Theorem 5.17. *Let $\pi : \bar{A} \times \bar{A} \to \mathbb{R}$ be a fitness function with extension to the domain $\Delta^2 \times \Delta^2$ as in (2.6). If $\sigma^* \in \Delta^2$ is efficient w.r.t. π, then σ^* is stable w.r.t. π.*

For any fitness function on $\bar{A} \times \bar{A}$ an efficient strategy always exists since Δ^2 is compact and the fitness function extended to $\Delta^2 \times \Delta^2$ is continuous (in particular, $\sigma \mapsto \pi(\sigma, \sigma)$ is a continuous map). The following existence result for stable populations is now an immediate consequence of Theorem 5.17.

Corollary 5.18. *For any fitness function $\pi : \bar{A} \times \bar{A} \to \mathbb{R}$ with extension to the domain $\Delta^2 \times \Delta^2$ as in (2.6) there exists a $\mathcal{T}_\mathcal{R}$-population $\mu_\mathcal{R} \in \mathcal{P}(\mathcal{T}_\mathcal{R})$ which is stable w.r.t. π.*

As discussed at full length in the introduction of this chapter, the finding in Corollary 5.18 is in contrast to Dekel et al.'s model with expected utility types ([14]) in which even for generic fitness functions on $\{A, B\} \times \{A, B\}$ with an efficient mixed strategy a stable population does not exist. Reducing our type space from Chap. 2 to those preference relations which satisfy betweenness in the first component still allows us to sustain existence of such a stable population in the 2 × 2 case.

Note that due to the excessive additional mathematical complexity of the model we can neither make an affirmative nor a negative statement for cases with more than two pure strategies and the restricted type space $\mathcal{T}_\mathcal{R}$. We rather refer to our general existence result for the type space $\mathcal{T}$ and for any finite number of pure strategies obtained in the second chapter.

A Model with Two Populations

A crucial assumption made in Sect. 2.3 is that the two agents for each match are drawn according to a single population and cannot observe their positions in the game they play. This modeling is justified by the symmetry of the fitness function. It is argued that both player positions have completely identical characteristics and that an agent's role is thus nonrelevant. Yet, other setups are certainly imaginable. One such modification is to assume that there are two populations, one for each position in the game, and that always agents according to both populations are matched in pairs. A second option is to stick to a one-population world but to require that each two agents drawn can identify their role and can condition their behavior on this observation. In this chapter we mainly concentrate on the first variant and sketch an approach for the second one. We do not aim at providing a full-fledged study as in the previous chapters. We rather develop a short outlook and check our earlier model for robustness, especially concerning the properties of stable strategies and their trend towards efficiency. Higher attention is paid to strategies than to the explicit differentiation between expected utility and non-expected utility preferences.

In Sect. 6.1 we describe how our concepts for the analysis of the evolution of general preferences can be formally arranged to the case with two separate populations. In particular, we propose a new stability concept which is intended to capture most of the substantial ideas from its one-population counterpart. We apply this modified model to some examples in Sect. 6.2. The material games studied resemble a coordination game, the prisoner's dilemma and an anti-coordination game. The purpose of the section is to study which strategy profiles, if any, may be stable in our two-population setup and how these findings differ from the results obtained for a single population. In Sect. 6.3

we briefly discuss how a setup with a single population but with role identification may be approached.

6.1 Two-Population Stability

The formal fundament of the interaction is identical to the one in the previous chapters. We consider a two-player strategic preform with n pure strategies for both players and assume that agents choose mixed strategies, i.e. further on their strategy space is given by Δ^n. Also, we continue to assume that the fitness function on pure strategy profile is symmetric and can be extended to mixed strategy profiles according to (2.6).

The innovation of this chapter is that agents which are matched to play a game are drawn according to two separate populations. A particular population exists for each player position. Yet, populations are defined exactly as in Definition 2.15 and neither this concept nor that of the type space requires any formal adjustment. Remember that a type is just a preference relation on strategy profiles. This includes the implicit assumption that an agent's preferences are independent of the position in the game.

As before it is assumed that in any match of two agents drawn according to the two populations a Nash equilibrium in terms of their preferences is played. Such an equilibrium naturally still exists since the type space has not been modified. The following definition extends the concept of an equilibrium configuration to the setup with two populations. The particular Nash equilibrium played is specified for any match of agents of types from the two populations.

Definition 6.1. Let μ^1 and μ^2 be populations with supports $C(\mu^1)$ and $C(\mu^2)$, respectively. A pair $((b_T^1)_{T \in C(\mu^1)}, (b_{T'}^2)_{T' \in C(\mu^2)})$ of families $(b_T^i)_{T \in C(\mu^i)}$ of functions $b_T^i : C(\mu^{3-i}) \to \Delta^n$, $T \in C(\mu^i)$, $i \in \{1, 2\}$ is called a two-population equilibrium configuration if for any $T' \in C(\mu^1)$, $T'' \in C(\mu^2)$ the strategy profile $(b_{T'}^1(T''), b_{T''}^2(T'))$ is a Nash equilibrium of the two-player strategic game $(N, (\Delta^n, \Delta^n), (\succsim_{T'}, \succsim_{T''}))$.

We denote the set of all possible two-population equilibrium configurations given μ^1 and μ^2 by $\bar{B}(\mu^1, \mu^2)$. For the purpose of keeping some expressions plain we may suppress the indices and abbreviate a typical element $((b_T^1)_{T \in C(\mu^1)}, (b_{T'}^2)_{T' \in C(\mu^2)})$ of $\bar{B}(\mu^1, \mu^2)$ by b. In order to accentuate its meaning as a strategy, we may also denote $b_T^i(T')$ by $\sigma_{TT'}^{bi}$. It is the (equilibrium) mixed strategy chosen by an agent of type T in player position i when matched with an agent of type T' under the two-population equilibrium configuration $b = ((b_T^1)_{T \in C(\mu^1)}, (b_{T'}^2)_{T' \in C(\mu^2)})$.

Given two populations μ^1 and μ^2 and a two-population equilibrium configuration $b = ((b_T^1)_{T \in C(\mu^1)}, (b_{T'}^2)_{T' \in C(\mu^2)}) \in \bar{B}(\mu^1, \mu^2)$, we can compute the average fitness of an agent of type $T^i \in C(\mu^i)$, $i \in \{1, 2\}$:

$$\Pi_{T^i}^i((\mu^1, \mu^2) \mid b) \equiv \sum_{T' \in C(\mu^{3-i})} \mu^{3-i}(T') \; \pi(b_{T^i}^i(T'), b_{T'}^{3-i}(T^i)). \qquad (6.1)$$

In the following definition we introduce a reasonably adapted stability concept for the current two-population model. To begin with, we present the formal version followed by a detailed discussion of its properties.

Definition 6.2. *Let $\pi : \bar{A} \times \bar{A} \to \mathbb{R}$ be a fitness function with extension to the domain $\Delta^n \times \Delta^n$ as in (2.6).*

a. *A triple (μ^1, μ^2, b), where $\mu^1, \mu^2 \in \mathcal{P}(\mathcal{T})$ and $b = ((b_T^1)_{T \in C(\mu^1)}, (b_{T'}^2)_{T' \in C(\mu^2)})$ in $\bar{B}(\mu^1, \mu^2)$, is two-population stable w.r.t. π if the following conditions hold:*
i. *For every $i \in \{1, 2\}$ and $T', T'' \in C(\mu^i)$ we have*

$$\Pi_{T'}^i((\mu^1, \mu^2) \mid b) = \Pi_{T''}^i((\mu^1, \mu^2) \mid b). \qquad (6.2)$$

ii. *There exists an $\epsilon' > 0$ such that for every $T^1, T^2 \in \mathcal{T}$, $\epsilon_1, \epsilon_2 \in (0, \epsilon')$, $T_{\mu^1} \in C(\mu^1)$, $T_{\mu^2} \in C(\mu^2)$ and $\bar{b} \in \bar{B}(((1 - \epsilon_i)\mu^i + \epsilon_i \, \delta_{T^i})_i \mid b)$ and $j \in \{1, 2\}$ we have that*

$$\Pi_{T_{\mu^j}}^j(((1 - \epsilon_i)\mu^i + \epsilon_i \, \delta_{T^i})_i \mid \bar{b})$$
$$< \Pi_{T^j}^j(((1 - \epsilon_i)\mu^i + \epsilon_i \, \delta_{T^i})_i \mid \bar{b}) \qquad (6.3)$$

implies

$$\Pi_{T_{\mu^{3-j}}}^{3-j}(((1 - \epsilon_i)\mu^i + \epsilon_i \, \delta_{T^i})_i \mid \bar{b})$$
$$> \Pi_{T^{3-j}}^{3-j}(((1 - \epsilon_i)\mu^i + \epsilon_i \, \delta_{T^i})_i \mid \bar{b}), \qquad (6.4)$$

where $\bar{B}(((1-\epsilon_i)\mu^i + \epsilon_i \, \delta_{T^i})_i \mid b) \equiv \{\tilde{b} \in \bar{B}(((1-\epsilon_i)\mu^i + \epsilon_i \, \delta_{T^i})_i) :$ For every $i \in \{1, 2\}$ and $T' \in C(\mu^i)$ we have $\tilde{b}_{T'}^i \mid_{C(\mu^{3-i})} = b_{T'}^i\}$.
b. *A pair of populations (μ^1, μ^2) with $\mu^1, \mu^2 \in \mathcal{P}(\mathcal{T})$ is two-population stable w.r.t. π if there exists a two-population equilibrium configuration $b = ((b_T^1)_{T \in C(\mu^1)}, (b_{T'}^2)_{T' \in C(\mu^2)})$ such that the triple (μ^1, μ^2, b) is two-population stable w.r.t. π.*

c. *A strategy profile* $(\sigma_s, \sigma'_s) \in \Delta^n \times \Delta^n$ *is two-population stable w.r.t.* π
   if there exists a triple (μ^1, μ^2, b) *which is two-population stable*
   w.r.t. π *and where for any* $T \in C(\mu^1)$ *and* $T' \in C(\mu^2)$ *we have*
   $b_T^1 = \sigma_s$ *and* $b_{T'}^2 = \sigma'_s$.

A bit of interpretation is certainly at order here. The main idea of
the stability concept for two populations in Definition 6.2 is analogous
to the one-population version introduced in Definition 2.19. Condition *i.* requires that all agents of types within each population must
receive the same average fitness from their interactions with agents
of types from the other population. Further, we must have an invasion barrier ϵ' such that no two mutant types (one such mutant for
either population) which enter with population shares of less than ϵ'
can simultaneously may generate a strictly higher average fitness than
at least one incumbent type in their respective populations. In other
words, if one of any two mutants yields a strictly higher average fitness
in the post-entry population than any incumbent, the other mutant
must necessarily generate an average fitness which is strictly less than
that for all incumbents in their population. This is formally stated in
condition *ii.*

In essence, we have introduced a novel stability concept in Definition 6.2. No such concept for the analysis of preference evolution with
two populations has been proposed so far. A main characteristic is that
we allow for bilateral mutations, i.e. for a mutant in each of the two
populations. This property is in line with several multi-population stability requirements in related models. In a complementary setup with
exclusively "non-atomic" type distributions (i.e. populations) and no
observability of preferences, appropriately defined neighborhoods of a
type distribution $\mu \equiv \mu^1 \times \mu^2$ are considered ([17]). The concept typically used in evolutionary game theory is that of a so-called asymmetric evolutionary stable strategy (AESS; [59]). In fact, Swinkels therein
considers strategy profiles rather than strategies. A strategy profile
$\sigma = (\sigma_1, \sigma_2)$ satisfies his conditions if there exists an invasion barrier
ϵ' such that for any other strategy profile $\sigma^e = (\sigma_1^e, \sigma_2^e)$ (i.e. the mutant profile) at least one σ_i receives a strictly higher fitness against the
the post-entry population $(1 - \epsilon)\, \sigma + \epsilon\, \sigma^e$ than σ_i^e as long as we have
$\epsilon \in (0, \epsilon')$. Our stability concept in Definition 6.2 is in the same spirit.

We require that for stability no mutant-type agents may ever simultaneously outperform incumbent-type agents according to the two
populations. Mutants must do better or equal in both populations in
order to successfully invade. We like to emphasize that asking for immu-

nity in both populations would be too hard to satisfy. A more extensive discussion is renounced here.

6.2 An Outlook with Some Illustrative Examples

In this section we analyze a number of examples in which the fitness values correspond to some well-known games such as coordination games, the prisoner's dilemma and anti-coordination games. Our objective is to identify strategy profiles that come into question as potential two-population stable strategy profiles. On a larger scale than before the focus is here on stable profiles rather than on particular preferences, regardless of whether they have an expected utility representation or not. Since the current chapter places emphasis on illustration, we only consider 2×2 games and dispense with more general investigations.

6.2.1 Coordination Games

We revisit the situation from Example 3.2 in which the material game is a pure coordination game. The fitness values are 'doubly symmetric' in such a manner that for every $a_i, a_j \in \bar{A}$ we have $\pi(a_i, a_j) = \pi(a_j, a_i)$.

Example 6.3. Consider a two-player strategic preform with two pure strategies, i.e. with $\bar{A} = \{A, B\}$, and let the fitness values be as in Table 6.1.

Table 6.1. Fitness Values in a coordination game

	A	B
A	10,10	0,0
B	0,0	1,1

The strategy sets of the two players are given by Δ^2, the set of probability distributions on $\{A, B\}$. The fitness values for mixed strategy profiles in $\Delta^2 \times \Delta^2$ can be computed according to (2.6).

The material game in Example 6.3, i.e. the strategic game in which the preferences of the two players are represented by the fitness function, has two Nash equilibria in pure strategies, the strategy profiles (A, A) and (B, B). Moreover, (A, A) yields a fitness of 10 and thus Pareto dominates the other Nash equilibrium (B, B) in terms of the fitness values. It generates the highest possible fitness for both players.

We are interested in finding two-population stable strategy profiles for this situation. The two pure Nash equilibria are natural candidates. We start with the Pareto-dominant equilibrium (A, A) and claim that this strategy profile is two-population stable with two monomorphic populations. In either population A is a dominant strategy for agents of the only type. In several proofs in Chap. 5 we have seen that such a type does indeed exist in our type space $\mathcal{T}$. Condition $i.$ in Definition 6.2 is trivially satisfied as there exists a single type in each population. In order to see that condition $ii.$ is also satisfied, fix $\epsilon' = \frac{1}{4}$ and take any $T^1, T^2 \in \mathcal{T}$ and $\epsilon_1, \epsilon_2 \in (0, \epsilon')$. That is, T^1 and T^2 are arbitrary mutants and the post-entry populations are given by $(1 - \epsilon_i)\,\delta_{T_A} + \epsilon_i\,\delta_{T^i}$, $i \in \{1, 2\}$, where T_A is the incumbent type with dominant strategy A. In each match of any two agents both players receive the same expected fitness because of the 'double symmetry' of the fitness values. Choose any post-entry two-population equilibrium configuration $\bar{b}$ and let x_{ij} denote the fitness received from a match of an incumbent of population i with an entrant of population j. Note that we must always have $i \neq j$ since no agent ever meets another agent from her own population. Furthermore, let z denote the fitness from a match of entrant-type agents from the two populations.

The average post-entry fitness in population 1 is:

$$\Pi_{T_A}^1(((1 - \epsilon_i)\,\delta_{T_A} + \epsilon_i\,\delta_{T^i})_i \mid \bar{b}) = (1 - \epsilon_2) \cdot 10 + \epsilon_2\,x_{12},$$
$$\Pi_{T^1}^1(((1 - \epsilon_i)\,\delta_{T_A} + \epsilon_i\,\delta_{T^i})_i \mid \bar{b}) = (1 - \epsilon_2)\,x_{21} + \epsilon_2\,z. \tag{6.5}$$

The difference between these two values, denoted by D^1, is given by

$$D^1 = 10 - x_{21} - \epsilon_2\,(10 + z - x_{12} - x_{21}). \tag{6.6}$$

The average post-entry fitness in population 2 is:

$$\Pi_{T_A}^2(((1 - \epsilon_i)\,\delta_{T_A} + \epsilon_i\,\delta_{T^i})_i \mid \bar{b}) = (1 - \epsilon_1) \cdot 10 + \epsilon_1\,x_{21},$$
$$\Pi_{T^2}^2(((1 - \epsilon_i)\,\delta_{T_A} + \epsilon_i\,\delta_{T^i})_i \mid \bar{b}) = (1 - \epsilon_1)\,x_{12} + \epsilon_1\,z. \tag{6.7}$$

The difference between these two values, denoted by D^2, is given by

$$D^2 = 10 - x_{12} - \epsilon_1\,(10 + z - x_{12} - x_{21}). \tag{6.8}$$

For the sum of D^1 and D^2 we obtain

$$D^1 + D^2 = 20 - x_{12} - x_{21} - \epsilon_1(10 + z - x_{12} - x_{21})$$
$$- \epsilon_2(10 + z - x_{12} - x_{21})$$
$$\geq 20 - x_{12} - x_{21} - \epsilon_1 (20 - x_{12} - x_{21}) \qquad (6.9)$$
$$- \epsilon_2 (20 - x_{12} - x_{21})$$
$$\geq 0$$

because we have $x_{12}, x_{21} \leq 10$ and $\epsilon_1 + \epsilon_2 \leq \frac{1}{2} < 1$. Yet, $D^1 + D^2$ can be positive only if D^1 or D^2 is positive (or both). If either one is strictly negative, the other one must be strictly positive. It follows that, if in either population the mutant is generating a strictly higher average fitness than the incumbent, then in the other population the mutant is necessarily strictly worse off. Therefore, this pair of monomorphic populations $(\delta_{T_A}, \delta_{T_A})$ is two-population stable with respect to the fitness values of Example 6.3. The latter in turn implies that the strategy profile (A, A) is two-population stable here.

In contrast, the other pure strategy Nash equilibrium, (B, B), is not two-population stable. In order to see this, consider two populations μ^1 and μ^2 with a two-population equilibrium configuration such that (B, B) is played in all matches. Take now as mutants for the two populations types T^1 and T^2 which are 'coordination preferences', i.e. such that A is a best response to A and B is a best response to B. We dispense with the proof that such types exist in the type space $\mathcal{T}$. Consider any two population shares ϵ_1 and ϵ_2 and suppose that under the post-entry two-population equilibrium configuration (B, B) is played in any match of a mutant-type agent with an incumbent-type agent. This is possible since this profile is a Nash equilibrium according to the preferences of the participating agents (remember that for any incumbent B is a best response to B). If two agents of the mutant types are matched they play (A, A). One easily verifies that for any $T_I^1 \in C(\mu^1), T_I^2 \in C(\mu^2)$ and $j \in \{1, 2\}$ we have

$$\Pi_{T_I^j}^j (((1 - \epsilon_i)\mu^i + \epsilon_i \, \delta_{T^i})_i \mid \bar{b})$$
$$= (1 - \epsilon_{3-j}) \cdot 1 + \epsilon_{3-j} \cdot 1 = 1,$$
$$\Pi_{T^j}^j (((1 - \epsilon_i)\mu^i + \epsilon_i \, \delta_{T^i})_i \mid \bar{b})$$
$$= (1 - \epsilon_{3-j}) \cdot 1 + \epsilon_{3-j} \cdot 10 > 1,$$

(6.10)

no matter how small ϵ_1 and ϵ_2 are. The mutants outperform the incumbents in both populations. Thus, the 'bad' Nash equilibrium (B, B) of the material game is not two-population stable with respect to the fitness values given in Example 6.3.

The latter two findings show that stability in the extension of our evolutionary model to two populations selects in favor of the Pareto-dominant Nash equilibrium. This result is similar to what we have seen in Sect. 3.2 for the one-population model and hence it emphasizes the robustness of our earlier setup. As has become apparent from the last paragraph, this property is due the fact that we had simultaneous mutations in both populations. If these entrant-type agents correlate to the efficient Nash equilibrium, then they may obtain a higher average fitness than the incumbent-type agents playing the inefficient equilibrium.

The current example shows that also in a two-population world not all Nash equilibria of the material game may be stable. In the next section we will investigate whether stability of at least some Nash equilibrium can be 'revived'. As we will see shortly, the result is negative and thus it confirms our one-population outcome as well.

6.2.2 The Prisoner's Dilemma

In our next example the material game is again a prisoner's dilemma. There is a slight difference in the fitness function compared to the one in Example 3.1.

Example 6.4. Consider a two-player strategic preform with two pure strategies, i.e. with $\bar{A} = \{A, B\}$, and let the fitness values be as in Table 6.2.

Table 6.2. Fitness values in Example 6.4

	A	B
A	3,3	0,4
B	4,0	1,1

The strategy sets of the two players are given by Δ^2, the set of probability distributions on $\{A, B\}$. The fitness values for mixed strategy profiles in $\Delta^2 \times \Delta^2$ can be computed according to (2.6).

In this example the pure strategy A ('Cooperation') is strictly dominated in terms of the fitness values by B ('Defection'). As is well known, the only Nash equilibrium of the material game is (B, B), the strategy profile in which both players choose to defect, i.e. they do not cooperate. Similar to Example 6.3 in the previous section we can show that this profile is not two-population stable: Consider two populations μ^1 and μ^2 with a two-population equilibrium configuration such that (B,B) is played in all matches. Take now as mutants for the two populations types T^1 and T^2 which are 'coordination preferences', i.e. such that A is a best response to A and B is a best response to B. Again, we dispense with the proof that such types exist in the type space $\mathcal{T}$. Consider any two population shares ϵ_1 and ϵ_2 and suppose that under the post-entry two-population equilibrium configuration the profile (B,B) is played in any match of a mutant-type agent with an incumbent-type agent. This is possible since this profile is a Nash equilibrium according to the preferences of the participating agent (remember that for any incumbent B is a best response to B). If two agents of the mutant types are matched they play (A,A). One easily verifies that for any $T_I^1 \in C(\mu^1)$, $T_I^2 \in C(\mu^2)$ and $j \in \{1,2\}$ we have

$$\Pi^j_{T_I^j}(((1-\epsilon_i)\mu^i + \epsilon_i\,\delta_{T^i})_i \mid \bar{b})$$
$$= (1-\epsilon_{3-j}) \cdot 1 + \epsilon_{3-j} \cdot 1 = 1,$$
$$\Pi^j_{T^j}(((1-\epsilon_i)\mu^i + \epsilon_i\,\delta_{T^i})_i \mid \bar{b})$$
$$= (1-\epsilon_{3-j}) \cdot 1 + \epsilon_{3-j} \cdot 3 > 1,$$

(6.11)

no matter how small ϵ_1 and ϵ_2 are. The mutants outperform the incumbents in both populations. Thus, the unique Nash equilibrium (B,B) of the material game is not two-population stable with respect to the fitness values given in Example 6.4.

A two-population stable strategy profile with respect to this fitness function yet exists, namely the profile (A,A). Stability is obtained with two monomorphic populations. In either population the unique type's best-response correspondence $\beta_{T_\sigma} : \Delta^2 \to \Delta^2$ is given by $\beta_{T_\sigma}(\sigma) = \{\sigma\}$. In the proof of Theorem 2.22 we have seen that such a type T_σ does indeed exist in our type space $\mathcal{T}$. Condition $i.$ in Definition 6.2 is trivially satisfied as there exists a single type in each population. In order to see that condition $ii.$ is also satisfied, fix $\epsilon' = \frac{1}{4}$ and let $T^1, T^2 \in \mathcal{T}$ and $\epsilon_1, \epsilon_2 \in (0, \epsilon')$. That is, T^1 and T^2 are arbitrary mutants and the post-entry populations are given by $(1-\epsilon_i)\,\delta_{T_\sigma} + \epsilon_i\,\delta_{T^i}$, $i \in \{1,2\}$. In each match with an incumbent-type agent both players must receive the same expected fitness because the Nash equilibrium (according to their preferences) played is necessarily a symmetric strategy profile. Choose any post-entry two-population equilibrium configuration $\bar{b}$ and let x_{ij} denote the fitness received from a match of an incumbent-type agent according to population i with an entrant-type agent according to population j. Note that we must always have $i \neq j$ since no agent ever meets another agent from her own population. Furthermore, let z_i denote the fitness of an entrant-type agent in position i from a match of two entrant-type agents.

The average post-entry fitness in population 1 is:

$$\Pi^1_{T_\sigma}(((1 - \epsilon_i)\,\delta_{T_\sigma} + \epsilon_i\,\delta_{T^i})_i \mid \bar{b}) = (1 - \epsilon_2) \cdot 3 + \epsilon_2\,x_{12},$$
$$\Pi^1_{T^1}(((1 - \epsilon_i)\,\delta_{T_\sigma} + \epsilon_i\,\delta_{T^i})_i \mid \bar{b}) = (1 - \epsilon_2)\,x_{21} + \epsilon_2\,z_1. \tag{6.12}$$

The difference between these two values, denoted by D^1, is given by

$$D^1 = 3 - x_{21} - \epsilon_2\,(3 + z_1 - x_{12} - x_{21}). \tag{6.13}$$

The average post-entry fitness in population 2 is:

$$\Pi^2_{T_\sigma}(((1 - \epsilon_i)\,\delta_{T_\sigma} + \epsilon_i\,\delta_{T^i})_i \mid \bar{b}) = (1 - \epsilon_1) \cdot 3 + \epsilon_1\,x_{21},$$
$$\Pi^2_{T^2}(((1 - \epsilon_i)\,\delta_{T_\sigma} + \epsilon_i\,\delta_{T^i})_i \mid \bar{b}) = (1 - \epsilon_1)\,x_{12} + \epsilon_1\,z_2. \tag{6.14}$$

The difference between these two values, denoted by D^2, is given by

$$D^2 = 3 - x_{12} - \epsilon_1\,(3 + z_2 - x_{12} - x_{21}). \tag{6.15}$$

For the sum of D^1 and D^2 we obtain

$$D^1 + D^2 = 6 - x_{12} - x_{21} - \epsilon_1\,(3 + z_1 - x_{12} - x_{21})$$
$$- \epsilon_2\,(3 + z_2 - x_{12} - x_{21}) \tag{6.16}$$
$$\geq 0$$

because we have $x_{12}, x_{21} \leq 3$ (remember that no symmetric strategy profile yields an expected fitness greater than three), $z_1 + z_2 \leq 6$ and $\epsilon_1 + \epsilon_2 \leq \frac{1}{2} < 1$. Yet, $D^1 + D^2$ can be positive only if D^1 or D^2 is positive (or both). If either one is strictly negative, the other one must be strictly positive. It follows that, if in either population the mutant is generating a strictly higher average fitness than the incumbent, then in the other population the mutant-type agents are necessarily strictly worse off. Therefore, this pair of monomorphic populations $(\delta_{T_\sigma}, \delta_{T_\sigma})$ is two-population stable with respect to the fitness values of Example 6.4. The latter in turn implies that the strategy profile (A, A) is two-population stable here.

6.2.3 An Anti-Coordination Game

At a first glance, the exposition of the previous two sections may indicate that two-population stability always selects in favor of strategies which are 'efficient' in the sense of Definition 2.20. In the two examples we have just discussed the strategy profile in which all agents use the efficient strategy is two-population stable. Yet, this fact is somewhat misleading. Efficiency as formerly used is not a senseful concept to work with in the model with two separate populations. The reason will become clear from the following example.

Example 6.5. Consider a two-player strategic preform with two pure strategies, i.e. with $\bar{A} = \{A, B\}$, and let the fitness values be as in Table 6.3.

Table 6.3. Fitness values in an anti-coordination game

	A	B
A	0,0	5,10
B	10,5	0,0

The strategy sets of the two players are given by Δ^2, the set of probability distributions on $\{A, B\}$. The fitness values for mixed strategy profiles in $\Delta^2 \times \Delta^2$ can be computed according to (2.6).

The material game in Example 6.5 is an anti-coordination situation. Both players wish to 'discoordinate' their choices but they disagree on the manner to do so. In the standard literature on game theory similar interactions are frequently referred to as hawk-dove games (or 'chicken' games).

The efficient strategy in the sense of Definition 2.20 is $\sigma^* = \frac{1}{2}$ yielding an expected fitness of 3.75. However, two populations μ^1 and μ^2 in which all agents received an average fitness of 3.75 would be easily invadable by mutants. Take now as mutants for the two populations types T^1 and T^2 which are 'discoordination preferences', i.e. such that A is a best response to B and B is a best response to A. Also, mutant-type agents must be able to immitate an arbitrary incumbent agent according to their respective population. Again, we dispense with the proof that such types exist in the type space $\mathcal{T}$. Consider any two population shares ϵ_1 and ϵ_2 and suppose that under the post-entry two-population equilibrium configuration a mutant-type agent immitates the behavior of an arbitrary incumbent-type agent according to its own population when matched with any incumbent agent. If two agents of the mutant types are matched they play (A, B). One easily verifies that for any $T_I^1 \in C(\mu^1)$, $T_I^2 \in C(\mu^2)$ we have

$$\Pi_{T_I^1}^1(((1 - \epsilon_i)\mu^i + \epsilon_i\,\delta_{T^i})_i \mid \bar{b})$$

$$= (1 - \epsilon_2) \cdot 3.75 + \epsilon_2 \cdot 3.75 = 3.75,$$

$$\Pi_{T^1}^1(((1 - \epsilon_i)\mu^i + \epsilon_i\,\delta_{T^i})_i \mid \bar{b})$$

$$= (1 - \epsilon_2) \cdot 3.75 + \epsilon_2 \cdot 5 > 3.75$$

(6.17)

and

$$\Pi_{T_I^2}^2(((1 - \epsilon_i)\mu^i + \epsilon_i\,\delta_{T^i})_i \mid \bar{b})$$

$$= (1 - \epsilon_1) \cdot 3.75 + \epsilon_1 \cdot 3.75 = 3.75,$$

$$\Pi_{T^2}^2(((1 - \epsilon_i)\mu^i + \epsilon_i\,\delta_{T^i})_i \mid \bar{b})$$

$$= (1 - \epsilon_1) \cdot 3.75 + \epsilon_1 \cdot 10 > 3.75$$

(6.18)

no matter how small ϵ_1 and ϵ_2 are. The mutants outperform the incumbents in both populations. The intuition is that in our model of Chap. 2 with a single population there was just one mutant type. Furthermore, these mutant-type agents could not condition their behavior on the position in the game. Sloppily speaking, we now have a 'row player mutant' and a 'column player mutant' which together can destabilize the strategy profile (σ^*, σ^*).

A two-population stable strategy profile with respect to this fitness function yet exists and it is in fact asymmetric. For instance, the profile (A, B) is two-population stable in this example. Stability is obtained with two monomorphic populations where pure strategy A (and B, respectively) is a dominant strategy for agents of the only type in population 1 (and 2 respectively). In several proofs in Chap. 5 we have seen that such types do indeed exist in our type space $\mathcal{T}$. Condition i. in Definition 6.2 is trivially satisfied as there exists a single type in each population. In order to see that condition ii. is also satisfied, fix $\epsilon' = \frac{1}{4}$ and let $T^1, T^2 \in \mathcal{T}$ and $\epsilon_1, \epsilon_2 \in (0, \epsilon')$. That is, T^1 and T^2 are arbitrary mutants and the post-entry populations are given by $(1 - \epsilon_1)\,\delta_{T_A} + \epsilon_1\,\delta_{T^1}$ and $(1 - \epsilon_2)\,\delta_{T_B} + \epsilon_2\,\delta_{T^2}$. Choose any post-entry two-population equilibrium configuration $\bar{b}$ and let x_{ij} denote the fitness that the position 1 player receives from a match of an incumbent of population i with an entrant of population j. It follows immediately that given the particular preferences of the incumbents the position 2 player always receives 2 x_{ij}. Note that we must always have $i \neq j$ since no agent ever meets another agent according to her own population. Furthermore, let z_i denote the fitness of an entrant-type agent in position i from a match of two entrant-type agents.

The average post-entry fitness in population 1 is

$$
\begin{aligned}
\Pi^1_{T_A}(((1-\epsilon_i)\,\delta_{T^i_I} + \epsilon_i\,\delta_{T^i})_i \mid \bar{b}) &= (1-\epsilon_2)\cdot 5 + \epsilon_2\,x_{12}, \\
\Pi^1_{T^1}(((1-\epsilon_i)\,\delta_{T^i_I} + \epsilon_i\,\delta_{T^i})_i \mid \bar{b}) &= (1-\epsilon_2)\,x_{21} + \epsilon_2\,z_1,
\end{aligned}
\tag{6.19}
$$

where $T^1_I = T_A$ and $T^2_I = T_B$. The difference between these two values, denoted by D^1, is given by

$$
D^1 = 5 - x_{21} - \epsilon_2\,(5 + z_1 - x_{12} - x_{21}).
\tag{6.20}
$$

The average post-entry fitness in population 2 is:

$$
\begin{aligned}
\Pi^2_{T_B}(((1-\epsilon_i)\,\delta_{T^i_I} + \epsilon_i\,\delta_{T^i})_i \mid \bar{b}) &= (1-\epsilon_1)\cdot 10 + 2\,\epsilon_1\,x_{21}, \\
\Pi^2_{T^2}(((1-\epsilon_i)\,\delta_{T^i_I} + \epsilon_i\,\delta_{T^i})_i \mid \bar{b}) &= 2\,(1-\epsilon_1)\,x_{12} + \epsilon_1\,z_2.
\end{aligned}
\tag{6.21}
$$

The difference between these two values, denoted by D^2, is given by

$$
D^2 = 10 - 2\,x_{12} - \epsilon_1\,(10 + z_2 - 2\,x_{12} - 2\,x_{21}).
\tag{6.22}
$$

For the sum of D^1 and D^2 we obtain

$$
\begin{aligned}
D^1 + D^2 &= 15 - 2\,x_{12} - x_{21} \\
&\quad - \epsilon_1\,(10 + z_2 - 2\,x_{12} - 2\,x_{21}) \\
&\quad - \epsilon_2\,(5 + z_1 - x_{12} - x_{21}) \\
&= 5\,(3 - 2\,\epsilon_1 - \epsilon_2) - x_{12}\,(2 - 2\,\epsilon_1 - \epsilon_2) \\
&\quad - x_{21}\,(1 - 2\,\epsilon_1 - \epsilon_2) - (\epsilon_2\,z_1 + \epsilon_1\,z_2) \\
&\geq 11.25 - 1.25\,x_{12} - 0.25\,x_{21} - 0.25\,(z_1 + z_2) \\
&\geq 11.25 - 6.25 - 1.25 - 3.75 \\
&= 0
\end{aligned}
\tag{6.23}
$$

because we have $x_{12}, x_{21} \in [0, 5]$ and $0 \leq z_1 + z_2 \leq 15$ and $\epsilon_1, \epsilon_2 \leq \frac{1}{4}$. Yet, $D^1 + D^2$ can be positive only if D^1 or D^2 is positive (or both). If either one is strictly negative, the other one must be strictly positive. It follows that, if in either population the mutant is generating a strictly higher average fitness than the incumbent, then in the other population the mutant-type agents are necessarily strictly worse off. Therefore, this pair of monomorphic populations $(\delta_{T_A}, \delta_{T_B})$ is two-population stable with respect to the fitness values given in Example 6.5. The latter in turn implies that the strategy profile (A, B) is two-population stable here. Analogously, one can show that the profile (B, A) is also two-population stable.

6.3 Asymmetric Contests

In this chapter we have replaced our earlier assumption that agents are drawn according to a single population and cannot identify their position in the game by a setup where the agents for the two positions are drawn according to separate populations. Another approach commonly pursued in the literature on evolutionary game theory (cf. [55] and [59]) is to assume that the two agents for each match come from a single population but are able to observe their position in the game. Mailath ([35]) compares such a setup with a situation in which one player acts as the "owner" and the other as the "visitor". We do not aim at debating which of these approaches seems appropriate in any particular environment. Yet, in the indicated model the interaction is usually "symmetrized" by imposing a move of nature that determines each player's position. In a match with an opponent an agent is allocated to either position with probability $\frac{1}{2}$ but as aforementioned it can correctly observe the outcome of this move. Hence, each agent can condition her behavior on this observation. A strategy for any match is now a pair (σ_1, σ_2) where σ_i is played when in position i. The expected fitness from the match can be calculated by taking the expectation of the expected fitness received in the two player positions.

Our model analyzing the evolution of preferences could also be adjusted to such a setup. However, preferences would then have to be defined on strategy profiles $((\sigma_1, \sigma_2), (\sigma_1', \sigma_2'))$, where σ_i is the own strategy used in position i and σ_j' is used by the opponent in position j. Due to the move of nature there is an additional ex-ante uncertainty about the position in the game. It does not seem obvious from a normative point of view what properties such preferences should have. Remember that we have assumed that preferences on strategy profiles need not have an expected utility representation in the case when the position is nonrelevant. Therefore, there is no reason to hypothesize that the utility from a strategy profile $((\sigma_1, \sigma_2), (\sigma_1', \sigma_2'))$ is necessarily that expectation of some utilities from (σ_1, σ_2') and (σ_2, σ_1') with probabilities $\frac{1}{2}$. One could certainly modify the concept of an equilibrium configuration: A configuration given any population μ would then be a familiy of functions $b_T : C(\mu) \to \Delta^n \times \Delta^n$ such that for any $T, T' \in C(\mu)$ the strategy profile $(b_T(T'), b_{T'}(T))$ is a Nash equilibrium according to the preferences T and T'. Yet, we reemphasize that these preference relations would need to be further characterized. We will not get further on with this outlook and abstain from providing any formal stability concept or subsequent results.

7

Conclusions

Numerous empirical studies have demonstrated that individual choice behavior in the context of risk and uncertainty is not consistent with von Neumann and Morgenstern's expected utility theory. The latter's central assumption, the independence axiom, is known to be systematically violated.

Despite these insights, expected utility theory has remained the standard underlying model of individual choice in economics, in particular in game theory. In contrast to theories in which the decisions of a single agent are analyzed, game theory considers interactions among agents. The field of evolutionary game theory tries to explain the selection of a particular strategy through evolutionary pressures. Each strategy available to an individual is assumed to yield a certain biological fitness which also depends on the strategies used by the agents the individual interacts with. The basic idea corresponds to Darwin's principle according to which only agents with the highest fitness may survive during the course of evolution. However, evolutionary game theory is not a full-fledged theory of choice. Agents do not base their behavior on any preferences they might have. They are rather genetically precommited to the use of a particular strategy.

This drawback of evolutionary game theory is tackled in the literature on evolution of preferences in which the 'indirect evolutionary approach' is followed. Agents have preferences on strategy profiles and choose optimally according to these preferences in all their interactions. Evolution then selects in favor of those preferences which yield the highest average fitness. Considering the above-mentioned weaknesses of von Neumann and Morgenstern's traditional theory, it appears unfavorable that in the vast majority of these works all preferences are assumed to have an expected utility representation.

The aim of this monograph was to study a setup with general, possibly non-expected utility preferences and to investigate properties of evolutionary stable populations in such a framework. A major feature of our model is that existence of such a stable population is guaranteed for any finite number of pure strategies available to the agents and an arbitrary fitness function. This is an important progress compared to most works in evolutionary game theory and on evolution of preferences. Moreover, we have shown that in the case of two pure strategies and generic fitness values a stable population must necessarily not include any type which has an expected utility representation. Other preferences yield a higher average fitness. This result emphasizes the need to include preferences which differ from the expected utility hypothesis in the model. We have formally described those kinds of preference relations which may potentially occur in the support of any stable population when expected utility preferences are evolutionarily disselected. Another important finding is that the strategy profiles chosen in stable populations need not coincide with Nash equilibria of the material game, i.e. the game with fitness maximizing players. This is in line with other models on evolution of preferences which also demonstrate a tendency towards efficient strategy profiles.

In addition, we have checked the robustness of the results with respect to different changes in the underlying assumptions. First, we have put some additional structure on our general type space by restricting it to those preference relations which satisfy some form of betweenness. As it has turned out, the existence result for stable populations still holds at least in the case of two pure strategies. In a second extension we have dispensed with the restriction that the agents for each match are drawn according to a single population. Yet, the trend towards some sort of efficient strategy profiles remains when the agents for the two positions in the game are randomly drawn and there is a separate population for each. Again, stability does not require that a Nash equilibrium of the material game is played.

In the extension of the model to the case with two populations we have provided a mathematical setup and a definition of an appropriately adapted stability concept. With some prominent examples such as the prisoner's dilemma, a coordination game and a hawk-dove game we have developed an understanding for its properties. A more formal analysis could be an interesting task for subsequent work. In our last section we have discussed the case of asymmetric contests in which the types of the two agents for each match are from the same population but the agents can condition their behavior on the position in the game.

A complete investigation could yield additional insights into issues on evolution of preferences.

Another possible direction of future research includes the possibility of noisy signals. In such a model the type of an agent's opponent is incorrectly observed with a certain, usually small probability. Thus, the agent's choice of a strategy may not only depend on the observed type of the opponent but also on the possibility of receiving a wrong signal. Moreover, one could model an incomplete information setting in which each agent can correctly observe the type of an opponent with some fixed probability and observes nothing otherwise. Some preliminary work has been done in this context but exclusively for expected utility preferences.

A

Proofs for Chapter 2

A.1 Proof of Proposition 2.21

Proof. Consider any map $t : C(\mu) \to C(\mu)$ such that

$$t(T) \in \underset{T' \in C(\mu)}{\text{argmax }} \pi(b_{T'}(T), b_T(T')). \tag{A.1}$$

That is, $t(T)$ is the incumbent type that generates the highest fitness in matches with agents of type T under the equilibrium configuration b. As $C(\mu)$ is a finite set, t is well-defined. Consider the mutant T_0 which is defined as the type where the agents are indifferent among all strategy profiles. Such a preference relation is trivially continuous and convex on the own strategy space. For the moment we hypothesize that T_0 is not already an element of $C(\mu)$. See the arguments below for the case in which this is not true. We take a post-entry equilibrium configuration $\bar{b}$ as follows. When a T_0 agent is matched against another T_0 agent an efficient strategy σ^* is played, i.e. we have $\bar{b}_{T_0}(T_0) = \sigma^*$. When matched with any incumbent $T \in C(\mu)$, the T_0 agent imitates the behavior of the incumbent-type agent which is most successful in terms of fitness values against the Ts. Formally, for any $T \in C(\mu)$ we set $\bar{b}_{T_0}(T) = b_{t(T)}(T)$ and $\bar{b}_T(T_0) = b_T(t(T))$. This is possible since T_0's best responses always contain the best responses of any other type.

For any incumbent $T \in C(\mu)$ the average post-entry fitness is then given by

$$
\begin{aligned}
\Pi_T((1 - \epsilon)\,\mu + \epsilon\,\delta_{T_0} \mid \bar{b}) \\
= (1 - \epsilon) \sum_{T' \in C(\mu)} \pi(b_T(T'), b_{T'}(T))\,\mu(T') \\
+ \epsilon\,\pi(b_T(t(T)), b_{t(T)}(T))),
\end{aligned} \tag{A.2}
$$

where ϵ is the mutant's population share. The average fitness of the mutant-type agents is

$$\Pi_{T_0}((1-\epsilon)\,\mu + \epsilon\,\delta_{T_0} \mid \bar{b})$$
$$= (1-\epsilon) \sum_{T' \in C(\mu)} \pi(b_{t(T')}(T'), b_{T'}(t(T')))\,\mu(T') + \epsilon\,\pi^*. \quad (A.3)$$

Note that for all $T, T' \in C(\mu)$, by definition,

$$\pi(b_T(T'), b_{T'}(T)) \leq \pi(b_{t(T')}(T'), b_{T'}(t(T'))) \quad (A.4)$$

holds. If there existed $\bar{T}, \bar{T}' \in C(\mu)$ such that

$$\pi(b_{\bar{T}}(\bar{T}'), b_{\bar{T}'}(\bar{T})) < \pi(b_{t(\bar{T}')}(\bar{T}'), b_{\bar{T}'}(t(\bar{T}'))), \quad (A.5)$$

then for sufficiently small $\epsilon > 0$ we would have $\Pi_{T_0}(.) > \Pi_{\bar{T}}(.)$, i.e. the entrant would yield a strictly higher fitness than at least one incumbent. As (μ, b) is stable w.r.t. π, this cannot occur. Hence, we must have

$$\forall\, T, T', T'' \in C(\mu): \ \pi(b_T(T'), b_{T'}(T)) = \pi(b_{T''}(T'), b_{T'}(T'')). \quad (A.6)$$

The first summands on the right-hand side in (A.2) and (A.3), respectively, must therefore be equal.

With the same argument we obtain that for any $T \in C(\mu)$ we have

$$\pi(b_T(t(T)), b_{t(T)}(T)) = \pi(b_{t(T)}(t(T)), b_{t(T)}(t(T))) \leq \pi^*. \quad (A.7)$$

The inequality in (A.7) follows from the fact that π^* is the highest fitness which can be received from a match with an agent of the same type. Remember that a symmetric Nash equilibrium must be played in any such match. By definition, the efficient strategy yields the highest fitness among all symmetric strategy profiles. Therefore, stability of (μ, b), together with the fitness in (A.2) and (A.3), implies that for any $T \in C(\mu)$ we have $\pi(b_T(t(T)), b_{t(T)}(T)) = \pi^*$.

As (A.6) shows, any map from $C(\mu)$ into itself satisfies (A.1). Hence, we obtain

$$\forall\, T, T' \in C(\mu): \ \pi(b_T(T'), b_{T'}(T)) = \pi^*. \quad (A.8)$$

This proves the claim. However, we still need to treat the case in which T_0 is already a member of the population, i.e. where $T_0 \in C(\mu)$. We can construct a mutant which is 'similar to T_0' (in the sense that it satisfies all the properties in terms of best responses of T_0 as above; we do not mean closeness in a topological sense) and which does not yet belong to $C(\mu)$. In order to do so let

$$\Delta_b^n \equiv \bigcup_{T \in C(\mu)} \operatorname{Im} b_T \cup \{\sigma^*\}, \tag{A.9}$$

where σ^* is the efficient strategy from above. Fix any $\bar{x} \in \Delta^n \backslash \Delta_b^n$. That is, $\bar{x}$ is a strategy which is not played by any agent of any type within the population μ in any Nash equilibrium according to the equilibrium configuration b.

Consider the utility function $u_{T_0^\epsilon} : \Delta^n \times \Delta^n \to \mathbb{R}$ defined by

$$u_{T_0^\epsilon}(\sigma_T, \sigma_{-T}) = \min\{1, \epsilon^{-1} \|(\sigma_T, \sigma_{-T}) - (e_n, \bar{x})\|_1\}, \tag{A.10}$$

where ϵ is sufficiently small such that, for all $\sigma_{-T} \in \Delta_b^n$ and $\sigma_T \in \Delta^n$, we have $u_{T_0^\epsilon}(\sigma_T, \sigma_{-T}) = 1$ and where the preference relation $\succsim_{T_0^\epsilon}$ defined by

$$\sigma' \succsim_{T_0^\epsilon} \sigma'' :\Longleftrightarrow u_{T_0^\epsilon}(\sigma') \geq u_{T_0^\epsilon}(\sigma'') \tag{A.11}$$

is not an element of $C(\mu)$. This can always be done because of the finiteness of $C(\mu)$. Even more formally, one could use the terminology $u_{T_0^\epsilon}^{\bar{x}}$ instead of $u_{T_0^\epsilon}$. We forbear from doing this in order to keep the notation as concise as possible. Nonetheless we would like to emphasize that the function obviously depends on the value of $\bar{x}$.

We have to show that T_0^ϵ is an element of the type space $\mathcal{T}$, i.e. that $\succsim_{T_0^\epsilon}$ is convex in the first component and continuous. Continuity follows immediately from the definition since $u_{T_0^\epsilon}$ is continuous. In order to prove convexity let $(\bar{\sigma}_T, \bar{\sigma}_{-T}) \in \Delta^n \times \Delta^n$ and suppose that $\sigma_T', \sigma_T'' \in \Delta^n$ satisfy $(\sigma_T', \bar{\sigma}_{-T}) \succsim_{T_0^\epsilon} (\bar{\sigma}_T, \bar{\sigma}_{-T})$ and $(\sigma_T'', \bar{\sigma}_{-T}) \succsim_{T_0^\epsilon} (\bar{\sigma}_T, \bar{\sigma}_{-T})$. Let $\alpha \in [0, 1]$.

1st case: $u_{T_0^\epsilon}(\bar{\sigma}_T, \bar{\sigma}_{-T}) = 1$. Then, we have

$$\begin{aligned}
\|(\alpha \, \sigma_T' &+ (1 - \alpha) \, \sigma_T'', \bar{\sigma}_{-T}) - (e_n, \bar{x})\|_1 \\
&= 2 \sum_{i=1}^{n-1} (\alpha \, \sigma_T'^i + (1 - \alpha)\sigma_T''^i) + \|\bar{\sigma}_{-T} - \bar{x}\|_1 \\
&= \alpha \left(2 \sum_{i=1}^{n-1} \sigma_T'^i + \|\bar{\sigma}_{-T} - \bar{x}\|_1 \right) \\
&\quad + (1 - \alpha)\left(2 \sum_{i=1}^{n-1} \sigma_T''^i + \|\bar{\sigma}_{-T} - \bar{x}\|_1 \right) \\
&= \alpha \, \|(\sigma_T', \bar{\sigma}_{-T}) - (e_n, \bar{x})\|_1 \\
&\quad + (1 - \alpha) \, \|(\sigma_T'', \bar{\sigma}_{-T}) - (e_n, \bar{x})\|_1 \\
&\geq \alpha \epsilon + (1 - \alpha) \epsilon = \epsilon.
\end{aligned} \tag{A.12}$$

Therefore, we have $u_{T_0^\epsilon}(\alpha\,\sigma_T' + (1-\alpha)\,\sigma_T'', \bar{\sigma}_{-T}) = 1$ and thus

$$(\alpha\,\sigma_T' + (1-\alpha)\,\sigma_T'', \bar{\sigma}_{-T}) \succsim_{T_0^\epsilon} (\bar{\sigma}_T, \bar{\sigma}_{-T}). \qquad (A.13)$$

2nd case: $u_{T_0^\epsilon}(\bar{\sigma}_T, \bar{\sigma}_{-T}) = a < 1$ for some a. Then, we have

$$
\begin{aligned}
&\|(\alpha\,\sigma_T' + (1-\alpha)\,\sigma_T'', \bar{\sigma}_{-T}) - (e_n, \bar{x})\|_1 \\
&= 2\sum_{i=1}^{n-1}(\alpha\,\sigma_T'^i + (1-\alpha)\sigma_T''^i) + \|\bar{\sigma}_{-T} - \bar{x}\|_1 \\
&= \alpha\,(2\sum_{i=1}^{n-1}\sigma_T'^i + \|\bar{\sigma}_{-T} - \bar{x}\|_1) \\
&\quad + (1-\alpha)(2\sum_{i=1}^{n-1}\sigma_T''^i + \|\bar{\sigma}_{-T} - \bar{x}\|_1) \\
&= \alpha\,\|(\sigma_T', \bar{\sigma}_{-T}) - (e_n, \bar{x})\|_1 \\
&\quad + (1-\alpha)\,\|(\sigma_T'', \bar{\sigma}_{-T}) - (e_n, \bar{x})\|_1 \\
&\geq \alpha\,a\,\epsilon + (1-\alpha)\,a\,\epsilon = a\,\epsilon.
\end{aligned}
\qquad (A.14)
$$

Therefore, we have $u_{T_0^\epsilon}(\alpha\,\sigma_T' + (1-\alpha)\,\sigma_T'', \bar{\sigma}_{-T}) \geq a$ and thus

$$(\alpha\,\sigma_T' + (1-\alpha)\,\sigma_T'', \bar{\sigma}_{-T}) \succsim_{T_0^\epsilon} (\bar{\sigma}_T, \bar{\sigma}_{-T}). \qquad (A.15)$$

The special characteristic of the mutant we have just constructed, T_0 or an appropriate T_0^ϵ, is that agents of this type can imitate any incumbent's behavior. For, in any match with an opponent of a type from the population μ who plays according to the equilibrium configuration function b, the mutant-type agent is indifferent among all possible (mixed) strategies and can thus mimic the play of the particular incumbent that is most successful (in terms of the fitness values) against the given opponent.

Note that we could have started with an entrant of an appropriate type T_0^ϵ without using T_0 at all. However, we find the latter type and the resulting behavior of the corresponding agents more intuitive than that of its 'approximation'. Thus, the second part of the proof shall just prove the validity of the arguments in case that T_0 is already an element of $C(\mu)$. $\qquad\square$

A.2 Proof of Theorem 2.22

Proof. In all following proofs in which we establish stability of a population μ (or a strategy etc.) we will only consider entrants from $\mathcal{T} \setminus C(\mu)$. It is clear that no type from a population where all agents receive the same expected fitness in all their matches can reproduce such that the corresponding agents subsequently strictly outperform any incumbent-type agent.

Consider a monomorphic population that consists of a single type T_σ inducing a best-response correspondence $\beta_{T_\sigma} : \Delta^n \to \Delta^n$ defined as follows:

$$\beta_{T_\sigma}(\sigma) = \{\sigma\} \quad \forall \sigma \in \Delta^n. \tag{A.16}$$

We need to show that this monomorphic population is well-defined, i.e. that there exists $T_\sigma \in \mathcal{T}$ with the best-response correspondence β_{T_σ} stated above. Intuitively, this is without controversy and the technical argument is as follows: Consider the utility function $u_{T_\sigma} : \Delta^n \times \Delta^n \to \mathbb{R}$ defined by

$$u_{T_\sigma}(\sigma_T, \sigma_{-T}) = -\|\sigma_T - \sigma_{-T}\|_1 . \tag{A.17}$$

Define a preference relation $\succsim_{T_\sigma}$ by

$$\sigma' \succsim_{T_\sigma} \sigma'' :\Longleftrightarrow u_{T_\sigma}(\sigma') \geq u_{T_\sigma}(\sigma''). \tag{A.18}$$

The fact that $\succsim_{T_\sigma}$ generates the best-response correspondence β_{T_σ} as defined in (A.16) is obvious. It remains to show that $\succsim_{T_\sigma}$ is convex in the first component and continuous. Continuity follows immediately from the definition since u_{T_σ} is continuous.

In order to prove convexity let $(\bar{\sigma}_T, \bar{\sigma}_{-T}) \in \Delta^n \times \Delta^n$ and suppose that $\sigma'_T, \sigma''_T \in \Delta^n$ satisfy $(\sigma'_T, \bar{\sigma}_{-T}) \succsim_{T_\sigma} (\bar{\sigma}_T, \bar{\sigma}_{-T})$ and $(\sigma''_T, \bar{\sigma}_{-T}) \succsim_{T_\sigma} (\bar{\sigma}_T, \bar{\sigma}_{-T})$. For any $\alpha \in [0, 1]$, we have

$$u_{T_\sigma}(\alpha\,\sigma'_T + (1-\alpha)\,\sigma''_T, \bar\sigma_{-T})$$

$$= -\sum_{i=1}^{n} |\alpha\,\sigma'^i_T + (1-\alpha)\,\sigma''^i_T - \bar\sigma^i_{-T}|$$

$$= -\sum_{i=1}^{n} |\alpha\,(\sigma'^i_T - \bar\sigma^i_{-T}) + (1-\alpha)\,(\sigma''^i_T - \bar\sigma^i_{-T})|$$

$$\geq -\sum_{i=1}^{n} \left(\alpha\,|\sigma'^i_T - \bar\sigma^i_{-T}| + (1-\alpha)\,|\sigma''^i_T - \bar\sigma^i_{-T}| \right) \qquad \text{(A.19)}$$

$$= -\alpha \sum_{i=1}^{n} |\sigma'^i_T - \bar\sigma^i_{-T}| - (1-\alpha) \sum_{i=1}^{n} |\sigma''^i_T - \bar\sigma^i_{-T}|$$

$$= \alpha\,u_{T_\sigma}(\sigma'_T, \bar\sigma_{-T}) + (1-\alpha)\,u_{T_\sigma}(\sigma''_T, \bar\sigma_{-T})$$

$$\geq \alpha\,u_{T_\sigma}(\bar\sigma_T, \bar\sigma_{-T}) + (1-\alpha)\,u_{T_\sigma}(\bar\sigma_T, \bar\sigma_{-T})$$

$$= u_{T_\sigma}(\bar\sigma_T, \bar\sigma_{-T}).$$

Therefore,

$$(\alpha\,\sigma'_T + (1-\alpha)\,\sigma''_T, \bar\sigma_{-T}) \succsim_{T_\sigma} (\bar\sigma_T, \bar\sigma_{-T}) \qquad \text{(A.20)}$$

holds and this establishes convexity in the first component.

Now, suppose that the equilibrium played in any match within this population is (σ^*, σ^*), i.e. we have $b_{T_\sigma}(T_\sigma) = \sigma^*$. We claim that σ^* is stable w.r.t. the fitness function π, with this monomorphic population.

Consider any entrant type, say T_e, into the population such that in the post-entry equilibrium configuration $\bar b$ the Nash equilibrium which is played between an entrant-type agent and an incumbent-type agent is $(\sigma_e, \sigma_i) \equiv (\bar b_{T_e}(T_\sigma), \bar b_{T_\sigma}(T_e))$ and the Nash equilibrium between two entrant-type agents is $(\sigma_3, \sigma_3) \equiv (\bar b_{T_e}(T_e), \bar b_{T_e}(T_e))$. The average fitness generated by the incumbent and the entrant are, respectively, given by

$$\Pi_{T_\sigma}((1-\epsilon)\,\delta_{T_\sigma} + \epsilon\,\delta_{T_e} \mid \bar b) = (1-\epsilon)\,\pi^* + \epsilon\,\pi(\sigma_i, \sigma_e) \qquad \text{(A.21)}$$

and

$$\Pi_{T_e}((1-\epsilon)\,\delta_{T_\sigma} + \epsilon\,\delta_{T_e} \mid \bar b) = (1-\epsilon)\,\pi(\sigma_e, \sigma_i) + \epsilon\,\pi(\sigma_3, \sigma_3). \qquad \text{(A.22)}$$

Due to T_σ preferences any Nash equilibrium that is played in any match with at least one agent of this type must necessarily be symmetric, i.e. $(\sigma_e, \sigma_i) = (\sigma_e, \sigma_e)$ needs to hold. It follows that

$$\pi(\sigma_e, \sigma_i) = \pi(\sigma_e, \sigma_e) \leq \pi^* \qquad \text{(A.23)}$$

holds. For $\epsilon \leq \frac{1}{2}$ we have

$\Pi_{T_\sigma}((1 - \epsilon)\, \delta_{T_\sigma} + \epsilon\, \delta_{T_e} \mid \bar{b})$

$$= (1 - \epsilon)\, \pi^* + \epsilon\, \pi(\sigma_e, \sigma_e)$$

$$\geq (1 - \epsilon)\, \pi(\sigma_e, \sigma_e) + \epsilon\, \pi^* \tag{A.24}$$

$$\geq (1 - \epsilon)\, \pi(\sigma_e, \sigma_e) + \epsilon\, \pi(\sigma_3, \sigma_3)$$

$$= \Pi_{T_e}((1 - \epsilon)\, \delta_{T_\sigma} + \epsilon\, \delta_{T_e} \mid \bar{b}),$$

independently of the values of σ_3, σ_i and σ_e.

Therefore, for any $T_e \notin C(\mu)$, $\epsilon \in (0, \frac{1}{2})$ and $\bar{b} \in B((1 - \epsilon)\, \delta_{T_\sigma} + \epsilon\, \delta_{T_e})$ the average fitness generated by an entrant T_e can never exceed that of the incumbent type T_σ since the former enters in sufficiently small proportion. $\qquad\square$

B

Proofs for Chapter 4

B.1 Proof of Theorem 4.1

Proof. Let σ^* be an efficient strategy w.r.t. π. In the remainder of the proof, all efficiency and stability properties are with respect to this given fitness function π. Since A is not efficient, B cannot be efficient either because we have assumed that $a \geq d$. Hence, $\sigma^* \in (0,1)$ holds. By definition, we have

$$\sigma^* \in \operatorname*{argmax}_{\sigma \in [0,1]} \sigma^2 \, a + \sigma \, (1-\sigma) \, (b+c) + (1-\sigma)^2 \, d, \qquad (\text{B.1})$$

which yields

$$\sigma^* = \frac{b+c-2d}{2(b+c-a-d)} \qquad (\text{B.2})$$

via the first-order condition. The latter condition is sufficient as, by assumption, σ^* is an interior solution. Therefore, σ^* is the unique efficient strategy.

First, we investigate the algebraic sign of

$$\sigma^* \, a + (1-\sigma^*) \, b - (\sigma^* \, c + (1-\sigma^*) \, d). \qquad (\text{B.3})$$

We have

$$
\begin{aligned}
\sigma^* \, a &+ (1-\sigma^*) \, b - (\sigma^* \, c + (1-\sigma^*) \, d) \\
&= \sigma^* \, (a+d-b-c) + b - d \\
&= \frac{1}{2} \frac{b+c-2d}{b+c-a-d} (a+d-b-c) + b - d \qquad (\text{B.4}) \\
&= \frac{1}{2} (-b-c+2d+2b-2d) \\
&= \frac{1}{2} (b-c).
\end{aligned}
$$

Hence, it follows that

$$\sigma^* \, a + (1 - \sigma^*) \, b > \sigma^* \, c + (1 - \sigma^*) \, d \quad \text{if } b > c \tag{B.5}$$

and

$$\sigma^* \, a + (1 - \sigma^*) \, b < \sigma^* \, c + (1 - \sigma^*) \, d \quad \text{if } b < c. \tag{B.6}$$

As

$$\sigma^* \, (\sigma^* \, a + (1 - \sigma^*) \, b) + (1 - \sigma^*) \, (\sigma^* \, c + (1 - \sigma^*) \, d) = \pi^* \tag{B.7}$$

by the definition of an efficient strategy, we must have

$$\sigma^* \, c + (1 - \sigma^*) \, d < \pi^* \quad \text{if } \ b > c \tag{B.8}$$

and

$$\sigma^* \, a + (1 - \sigma^*) \, b < \pi^* \quad \text{if } \ b < c. \tag{B.9}$$

Second, we investigate the algebraic sign of

$$\sigma^* \, a + (1 - \sigma^*) \, c - (\sigma^* \, b + (1 - \sigma^*) \, d). \tag{B.10}$$

We have

$$
\begin{aligned}
\sigma^* \, a & + (1 - \sigma^*) \, c - (\sigma^* \, b + (1 - \sigma^*) \, d) \\
&= \sigma^* \, (a + d - b - c) + c - d \\
&= \frac{1}{2} \frac{b + c - 2d}{b + c - a - d} \, (a + d - b - c) + c - d \\
&= \frac{1}{2} \, (-b - c + 2d + 2c - 2d) \\
&= \frac{1}{2} \, (c - b).
\end{aligned}
\tag{B.11}
$$

Hence, it follows that

$$\sigma^* \, a + (1 - \sigma^*) \, c > \sigma^* \, b + (1 - \sigma^*) \, d \quad \text{if } b < c \tag{B.12}$$

and

$$\sigma^* \, a + (1 - \sigma^*) \, c < \sigma^* \, b + (1 - \sigma^*) \, d \quad \text{if } b > c. \tag{B.13}$$

By the definition of σ^*, the following equation must hold:

$$
\begin{aligned}
\sigma^* \, (\sigma^* \, a & + (1 - \sigma^*) \, c) + (1 - \sigma^*) \, (\sigma^* \, b + (1 - \sigma^*) \, d) \\
&= \sigma^* \, (\sigma^* \, a + (1 - \sigma^*) \, b) + (1 - \sigma^*) \, (\sigma^* \, c + (1 - \sigma^*) \, d) \\
&= \pi^*.
\end{aligned}
\tag{B.14}
$$

We must therefore have

$$\sigma^* \, b + (1 - \sigma^*) \, d > \pi^* \quad \text{if} \ \ b > c \tag{B.15}$$

and

$$\sigma^* \, a + (1 - \sigma^*) \, c > \pi^* \quad \text{if} \ \ b < c. \tag{B.16}$$

Let μ be a population and $b = (b_T)_{T \in C(\mu)}$ an equilibrium configuration such that the pair (μ, b) is stable. Proposition 2.21 implies that for all $T, T' \in C(\mu)$ the equation

$$\Pi_T(\mu \mid b) = \pi(b_T(T'), b_{T'}(T))) = \pi^* \tag{B.17}$$

holds. Hence, for any $T, T' \in C(\mu)$ we must have

$$\begin{aligned}
\pi^* &= \pi(b_T(T'), b_{T'}(T)) \\
&= \sigma^b_{TT'}(\sigma^b_{T'T} \, a + (1 - \sigma^b_{T'T}) \, b) \\
&\quad + (1 - \sigma^b_{TT'})(\sigma^b_{T'T} \, c + (1 - \sigma^b_{T'T}) \, d)
\end{aligned} \tag{B.18}$$

and

$$\begin{aligned}
\pi^* &= \pi(b_{T'}(T), b_T(T')) \\
&= \sigma^b_{TT'}(\sigma^b_{T'T} \, a + (1 - \sigma^b_{T'T}) \, c) \\
&\quad + (1 - \sigma^b_{TT'})(\sigma^b_{T'T} \, b + (1 - \sigma^b_{T'T}) \, d).
\end{aligned} \tag{B.19}$$

As $b \neq c$ the equalities in (B.18) and (B.19) can hold simultaneously only if

$$\sigma^b_{TT'}(1 - \sigma^b_{T'T}) = (1 - \sigma^b_{TT'})\sigma^b_{T'T} \tag{B.20}$$

which requires $\sigma^b_{TT'} = \sigma^b_{T'T}$. Since (σ^*, σ^*) is the only symmetric strategy profile which generates the fitness π^*, it must necessarily be the Nash equilibrium which is played in all matches within this population. That is, for all $T, T' \in C(\mu)$ we have $b_T(T') = \sigma^*$.

For the purpose of contradiction, suppose that $C(\mu)$ contains at least one type T_{EU} which has an expected utility representation. That is, the preference relation $\succsim_{T_{EU}}$ on $\Delta \times \Delta$ satisfies the von Neumann-Morgenstern axioms. As $T_{EU} \in C(\mu)$ we must have $\mu_{EU} \equiv \mu(T_{EU}) > 0$.

In particular, we must have $\sigma^* \in \beta_{T_{EU}}(\sigma^*)$, where $\beta_{T_{EU}}$ is the induced best-response correspondence. As $\sigma^* \in (0, 1)$ and since T_{EU} has an expected utility representation, it follows that $\beta_{T_{EU}}$ has one of the following functional forms:

$$\beta_{T_{EU}}(\sigma) = \begin{cases} \{1\} & \text{if } \sigma > \sigma^* \\ [0,1] & \text{if } \sigma = \sigma^* \\ \{0\} & \text{if } \sigma < \sigma^* \end{cases} \qquad (B.21)$$

$$\beta_{T_{EU}}(\sigma) = \begin{cases} \{0\} & \text{if } \sigma > \sigma^* \\ [0,1] & \text{if } \sigma = \sigma^* \\ \{1\} & \text{if } \sigma < \sigma^* \end{cases} \qquad (B.22)$$

or

$$\beta_{T_{EU}}(\sigma) = [0,1] \quad \text{for all } \sigma \in [0,1]. \qquad (B.23)$$

A type inducing the latter best-response correspondence will be denoted by T_0. The corresponding agents are indifferent among all mixed strategies for any mixed strategy of the opponent.

There are two possible cases:

1st case: $b > c$. Assume that T_0 enters (see the arguments below for the case in which T_0 is already an element of $C(\mu)$) with population share $\epsilon > 0$ and that in the post-entry population we have $\bar{b}_{T_{EU}}(T_0) = 0$ and $\bar{b}_{T_0}(T_{EU}) = \bar{b}_{T_0}(T_0) = \sigma^*$ (remember that every mixed strategy profile is a Nash equilibrium in the game with two players of type T_0). Further assume that in all matches with any agent of a third type, if one exists, the T_0 agent's choice duplicates the behavior of an arbitrary incumbent $\bar{T} \in C(\mu)\backslash\{T_{EU}\}$. That is, the Nash equilibria in the T_0 agent's matches with all incumbents other than the T_{EU} agents correspond to the Nash equilibria in the $\bar{T}$ agents' matches which we have seen to be necessarily (σ^*, σ^*). As the fitness from these matches is always π^*, we have for all $T \in C(\mu) \setminus \{T_{EU}\}$ if one exists,

$$\Pi_T((1-\epsilon)\,\mu + \epsilon\,\delta_{T_0} \mid \bar{b}) = \pi^*. \qquad (B.24)$$

Also, by (B.8), we obtain

$$\Pi_{T_{EU}}((1-\epsilon)\,\mu + \epsilon\,\delta_{T_0} \mid \bar{b})$$
$$= (1-\epsilon)\,\pi^* + \epsilon\,(\sigma^* c + (1-\sigma^*)\,d) \qquad (B.25)$$
$$< \pi^*$$

and (B.15) yields

$$\Pi_{T_0}((1-\epsilon)\,\mu + \epsilon\,\delta_{T_0} \mid \bar{b})$$

$$= (1 - (1-\epsilon)\,\mu_{EU})\,\pi^*$$

$$+ (1-\epsilon)\,\mu_{EU}\,(\sigma^* b + (1-\sigma^*)\,d) \tag{B.26}$$

$$> \pi^*.$$

The latter two inequalities hold for any $\epsilon > 0$. This means that no matter in what small proportion T_0 enters, it always yields a higher average fitness than T_{EU}. This contradicts the assumption that the pair (μ, b) is stable.

2nd case: $b < c$. Assume that T_0 enters with population share $\epsilon > 0$ and that in the post-entry population we have $\bar{b}_{T_{EU}}(T_0) = 1$ and $\bar{b}_{T_0}(T_{EU}) = \bar{b}_{T_0}(T_0) = \sigma^*$ (remember that every mixed strategy profile is a Nash equilibrium in the game with two players of type T_0). Further assume that in all matches with any agent of a third type, if one exists, the T_0 agent's choice duplicates the behavior of an arbitrary incumbent $\bar{T} \in C(\mu) \setminus \{T_{EU}\}$. That is, the Nash equilibria in the T_0 agent's matches with all incumbents other than the T_{EU} agents correspond to the Nash equilibria in the $\bar{T}$ agents' matches which we have seen to be necessarily (σ^*, σ^*). As the fitness from these matches is always π^*, we have for all $T \in C(\mu) \setminus \{T_{EU}\}$, if one exists,

$$\Pi_T((1-\epsilon)\,\mu + \epsilon\,\delta_{T_0} \mid \bar{b}) = \pi^*. \tag{B.27}$$

Also, by (B.9), we obtain

$$\Pi_{T_{EU}}((1-\epsilon)\,\mu + \epsilon\,\delta_{T_0} \mid \bar{b})$$

$$= (1-\epsilon)\,\pi^* + \epsilon\,(\sigma^* a + (1-\sigma^*)\,b) \tag{B.28}$$

$$< \pi^*$$

and (B.16) yields

$$\Pi_{T_0}((1-\epsilon)\,\mu + \epsilon\,\delta_{T_0} \mid \bar{b})$$

$$= (1 - (1-\epsilon)\,\mu_{EU})\,\pi^*$$

$$+ (1-\epsilon)\,\mu_{EU}\,(\sigma^* a + (1-\sigma^*)\,c) \tag{B.29}$$

$$> \pi^*.$$

The latter two inequalities hold for any $\epsilon > 0$. That means that no matter in what small proportion T_0 enters, it always yields a higher average fitness than T_{EU}. This contradicts the assumption that the pair (μ, b) is stable.

For technical reasons, in case that T_0 already exists in the population, we have to assume that a type which is 'similar to T_0' (in the following sense) enters: Select $\epsilon \in (0, 1)$ such that no type with a best-response correspondence $\beta_{T_0^\epsilon}$ defined by

$$\beta_{T_0^\epsilon}(\sigma) = [0, \min\{1, 1 + \epsilon + (1 - \epsilon)\,\sigma^* - \sigma\}] \tag{B.30}$$

already exists in the population. The finiteness of $C(\mu)$ ensures that this can be done. T_0^ϵ agents are indifferent among all strategies for any strategy played in any Nash equilibrium in the population μ (which is just σ^* as we have seen). A preference relation in $\mathcal{T}$ that satisfies our continuity and convexity assumptions and that induces this particular best-response correspondence can be constructed as follows: Consider the utility function $u_{T_0^\epsilon} : \Delta \times \Delta \to \mathbb{R}$ with

$$u_{T_0^\epsilon}(\sigma_T, \sigma_{-T}) = \min\{0, 1 + \epsilon + (1 - \epsilon)\sigma^* - \sigma_T - \sigma_{-T}\} \tag{B.31}$$

and define a preference relation $\succsim_{T_0^\epsilon}$ on $\Delta \times \Delta$ by

$$\bar{\sigma} \succsim_{T_0^\epsilon} \bar{\bar{\sigma}} :\Longleftrightarrow u_{T_0^\epsilon}(\bar{\sigma}) \geq u_{T_0^\epsilon}(\bar{\bar{\sigma}}). \tag{B.32}$$

This preference relation induces the best-response correspondence $\beta_{T_0^\epsilon}$. Continuity of $\succsim_{T_0^\epsilon}$ follows immediately from the continuity of $u_{T_0^\epsilon}$. Furthermore, $u_{T_0^\epsilon}$ is monotonically decreasing in the first component. Hence, $\succsim_{T_0^\epsilon}$ is convex in the first component. The direct proof goes as follows: Let $(\bar{\sigma}_T, \bar{\sigma}_{-T}) \in \Delta \times \Delta$ and suppose that $\sigma'_T, \sigma''_T \in \Delta$ satisfy $(\sigma'_T, \bar{\sigma}_{-T}) \succsim_{T_0^\epsilon} (\bar{\sigma}_T, \bar{\sigma}_{-T})$ and $(\sigma''_T, \bar{\sigma}_{-T}) \succsim_{T_0^\epsilon} (\bar{\sigma}_T, \bar{\sigma}_{-T})$. Let $\alpha \in [0, 1]$.

1st case: $u_{T_0^\epsilon}(\bar{\sigma}_T, \bar{\sigma}_{-T}) = 0$. Then, we must necessarily have

$$u_{T_0^\epsilon}(\sigma'_T, \bar{\sigma}_{-T}) = u_{T_0^\epsilon}(\sigma''_T, \bar{\sigma}_{-T}) = 0 \tag{B.33}$$

which implies

$$\begin{aligned}
1 &+ \epsilon + (1 - \epsilon)\sigma^* - (\alpha\sigma'_T + (1 - \alpha)\sigma''_T) - \bar{\sigma}_{-T} \\
&= \alpha\,(1 + \epsilon + (1 - \epsilon)\sigma^* - \sigma'_T - \bar{\sigma}_{-T}) \\
&\quad + (1 - \alpha)\,(1 + \epsilon + (1 - \epsilon)\sigma^* - \sigma''_T - \bar{\sigma}_{-T}) \\
&\geq \alpha\,0 + (1 - \alpha)\,0 \\
&= 0.
\end{aligned} \tag{B.34}$$

Therefore, we have $u_{T_0^\epsilon}(\alpha\, \sigma'_T + (1-\alpha)\, \sigma''_T, \bar{\sigma}_{-T}) = 0$ and thus

$$(\alpha\, \sigma'_T + (1-\alpha)\, \sigma''_T, \bar{\sigma}_{-T}) \succsim_{T_0^\epsilon} (\bar{\sigma}_T, \bar{\sigma}_{-T}). \qquad (B.35)$$

2nd case: $u_{T_0^\epsilon}(\bar{\sigma}_T, \bar{\sigma}_{-T}) = a < 0$ for some $a \in \mathbb{R}$. Then,

$$1 + \epsilon + (1-\epsilon)\sigma^* - (\alpha\sigma'_T + (1-\alpha)\sigma''_T) - \bar{\sigma}_{-T}$$

$$= \alpha\, (1 + \epsilon + (1-\epsilon)\sigma^* - \sigma'_T - \bar{\sigma}_{-T})$$

$$\qquad + (1-\alpha)\, (1 + \epsilon + (1-\epsilon)\sigma^* - \sigma''_T - \bar{\sigma}_{-T}) \qquad (B.36)$$

$$\geq \alpha\, a + (1-\alpha)\, a$$

$$= a$$

holds. Therefore, we have $u_{T_0^\epsilon}(\alpha\, \sigma'_T + (1-\alpha)\, \sigma''_T, \bar{\sigma}_{-T}) \geq a$ and thus

$$(\alpha\, \sigma'_T + (1-\alpha)\, \sigma''_T, \bar{\sigma}_{-T}) \succsim_{T_0^\epsilon} (\bar{\sigma}_T, \bar{\sigma}_{-T}). \qquad (B.37)$$

Hence, $\succsim_{T_0^\epsilon}$ is convex in the first component. Therefore, T_0^ϵ is an element of our type space $\mathcal{T}$. □

B.2 Proof of Theorem 4.2

Proof. Let μ be a stable population. In the remainder of the proof, all efficiency and stability properties are with respect to the given fitness function π. We have already seen in the discussion preceding the statement of Theorem 4.2 that for all $T \in C(\mu)$ we must have $\sigma^* \in \beta_T(\sigma^*)$, where β_T as usually denotes a T agent's best-response correspondence.

Since A is not efficient, B cannot be efficient either because we have assumed that $a \geq d$. Hence, it follows that $\sigma^* \in (0,1)$. By definition and since σ^* is unique, we have

$$\{\sigma^*\} = \underset{\sigma \in [0,1]}{\text{argmax}}\ \sigma^2\, a + \sigma(1-\sigma)\, (b+c) + (1-\sigma)^2\, d. \qquad (B.38)$$

The first-order condition is

$$2a\, \sigma^* + (b+c)\, (1-2\sigma^*) - 2d\, (1-\sigma^*) = 0 \qquad (B.39)$$

and the second-order condition requires

$$2a - 2(b+c) + 2d < 0. \qquad (B.40)$$

Since no pure strategy is efficient, σ^* is uniquely determined and we have

$$\sigma^* = \frac{b + c - 2d}{2(b + c - a - d)}. \tag{B.41}$$

However, (B.40) shows that σ^* maximizes the term on the right-hand side in (B.38) if and only if the fitness values satisfy $b + c > a + d \geq 2d$.

If there was a type $\bar{T} \in C(\mu)$ and a strategy profile $(\sigma'_{\bar{T}}, \sigma'_e)$ with $\sigma'_{\bar{T}} \in \beta_{\bar{T}}(\sigma'_e)$ and $\pi(\sigma'_e, \sigma'_{\bar{T}}) > \pi^*$, then an appropriate type, e.g. T_0, could successfully enter the population in a sufficiently small proportion if the corresponding agents play the Nash equilibrium $(\sigma'_e, \sigma'_{\bar{T}})$ when matched with an incumbent agent of type $\bar{T}$ while imitating an arbitrary incumbent-type agent's behavior in all other matches, if these exist. For any $T \in C(\mu)$, $\bar{\sigma}_e \in \Delta$ and $\sigma_T \in \beta_T(\bar{\sigma}_e)$ we must therefore have

$$\pi^* \geq \pi(\bar{\sigma}_e, \sigma_T)$$

$$= \bar{\sigma}_e \left(\sigma_T\, a + (1 - \sigma_T)\, b\right) + (1 - \bar{\sigma}_e) \left(\sigma_T\, c + (1 - \sigma_T)\, d\right)$$

$$= \sigma_T \left(\bar{\sigma}_e\, a + (1 - \bar{\sigma}_e)\, c\right) + (1 - \sigma_T) \left(\bar{\sigma}_e\, b + (1 - \bar{\sigma}_e)\, d\right) \tag{B.42}$$

$$= \sigma_T \left(\bar{\sigma}_e\, (a + d - b - c) + c - d\right) + \bar{\sigma}_e\, (b - d) + d$$

which is equivalent to

$$\sigma_T \left(\bar{\sigma}_e\, (a + d - b - c) + c - d\right) \leq \pi^* - d - \bar{\sigma}_e\, (b - d). \tag{B.43}$$

This implies that a necessary condition for stability is

$$\beta_T(\sigma_e) \subseteq \begin{cases} \left[0, \min\left\{1, \frac{\pi^* - d - \sigma_e (b-d)}{\sigma_e (a+d-b-c)+c-d}\right\}\right] & \text{if } \sigma_e < \frac{c-d}{b+c-a-d} \\ [0,1] & \text{if } \sigma_e = \frac{c-d}{b+c-a-d} \\ \left[\max\left\{0, \frac{\pi^* - d - \sigma_e (b-d)}{\sigma_e (a+d-b-c)+c-d}\right\}, 1\right] & \text{if } \sigma_e > \frac{c-d}{b+c-a-d} \end{cases} \tag{B.44}$$

These intervals are always non-empty: B is not efficient and 0 is therefore permitted as a best response to 0. Moreover, the function

$$x \mapsto \frac{\pi^* - d - x\,(b - d)}{x\,(a + d - b - c) + c - d} \tag{B.45}$$

is strictly increasing on $[0, \frac{c-d}{b+c-a-d})$ (for, the derivative of this function on $(0, \frac{c-d}{b+c-a-d})$ is

$$\frac{(b - c)^2}{(x\,(a + d - b - c) + c - d)^2} \tag{B.46}$$

which is strictly positive since $b \neq c$), which implies that it is always positive on this interval. This function is likewise strictly increasing on $(\frac{c-d}{b+c-a-d}, 1]$ and 1 is permitted as a best response to itself as A is not efficient, which implies that its values are always less than one on $(\frac{c-d}{b+c-a-d}, 1]$.

Note that $\frac{c-d}{b+c-a-d}$ could well be strictly larger than one, depending on whether $b - a$ is negative or not. If so, then the third case in (B.44) does obviously not apply. In the same manner, $\frac{c-d}{b+c-a-d}$ could also be strictly less than zero, depending on whether $c - d$ is negative or not. If so, then the first case in (B.44) does not apply.

In order to further characterize the set of stable populations we investigate the cases in which the entrant-type agents receive an expected fitness of exactly the efficient fitness π^* from a match with an incumbent-type agent. As one can see from (B.42) this occurs exactly for strategy profiles $(\sigma_T, \sigma_e) \in \Delta \times \Delta$ with

$$\sigma_T = \frac{\pi^* - d - \sigma_e(b - d)}{\sigma_e(a + d - b - c) + c - d}, \quad \sigma_e \neq \frac{c - d}{b + c - a - d}. \tag{B.47}$$

Equality in (B.42) can never occur when σ_e is equal to $\frac{c-d}{b+c-a-d}$ as this is not an efficient strategy. For, we have that

$$\frac{c - d}{b + c - a - d} - \sigma^* = \frac{c - d}{b + c - a - d} - \frac{b + c - 2d}{2(b + c - a - d)}$$

$$= \frac{c - b}{2(b + c - a - d)} \tag{B.48}$$

$$\neq 0$$

as $b \neq c$. The incumbent agent's expected fitness is given by

$$\pi(\sigma_T, \bar{\sigma}_e) = \sigma_T \left(\bar{\sigma}_e \, a + (1 - \bar{\sigma}_e) \, b \right)$$

$$+ (1 - \sigma_T) \left(\bar{\sigma}_e \, c + (1 - \bar{\sigma}_e) \, d \right) \tag{B.49}$$

$$= \sigma_T \left(\bar{\sigma}_e \, (a + d - b - c) + b - d \right) + \bar{\sigma}_e \, (c - d) + d.$$

Consider the function $g : [0,1] \setminus \{\frac{c-d}{b+c-a-d}\} \to \mathbb{R}$ defined by

$$g(x) = \frac{\pi^* - d - x \, (b - d)}{x \, (a + d - b - c) + c - d} \left(x \, (a + d - b - c) + b - d \right)$$

$$+ x \, (c - d) + d - \pi^*. \tag{B.50}$$

If $\frac{c-d}{b+c-a-d} \in [0, 1]$, then the function g has a vertical asymptote at $x = \frac{c-d}{b+c-a-d}$. The zeros of g are identical to those of

$$g(x) \ (x \ (a + d - b - c) + c - d) \tag{B.51}$$

which are the solutions to

$$
\begin{aligned}
0 &= (\pi^* - d - x \ (b - d)) \ (x \ (a + d - b - c) + b - d) \\
&\quad + (x \ (a + d - b - c) + c - d) \ (x \ (c - d) + d - \pi^*) \\
&= (\pi^* - d) \ (b - c) + x \ ((c - d)^2 - (b - d)^2) \\
&\quad + x^2 \ (c - b) \ (a + d - b - c)
\end{aligned} \tag{B.52}
$$

or equivalently to

$$
\begin{aligned}
0 &= \frac{(\pi^* - d) \ (b - c)}{(c - b) \ (a + d - b - c)} + \frac{(c - d)^2 - (b - d)^2}{(c - b) \ (a + d - b - c)} \, x + x^2 \\
&= \frac{\frac{(b + c - 2d)^2}{4(b + c - a - d)}}{b + c - a - d} - \frac{(c - b) \ (b + c - 2d)}{(c - b) \ (b + c - a - d)} \, x + x^2 \\
&= \frac{(b + c - 2d)^2}{4 \ (b + c - a - d)^2} - \frac{b + c - 2d}{b + c - a - d} \, x + x^2.
\end{aligned} \tag{B.53}
$$

Note that we have $b + c > a + d$ and $b \neq c$. Further, we have used that

$$
\begin{aligned}
\pi^* &= (\sigma^*)^2 \ a + \sigma^* (1 - \sigma^*) \ (b + c) + (1 - \sigma^*)^2 \ d \\
&= \frac{(b + c - 2d)^2}{4(b + c - a - d)} + d.
\end{aligned} \tag{B.54}
$$

Hence, g has a double null at $x = \frac{b + c - 2d}{2(b + c - a - d)} = \sigma^*$ and no other null.

We consider the following cases:

1st case: $b > c$. As $b + c > a + d$ and A and B are not efficient we must have $b > \pi^* > a \geq d$. Hence, the third case in (B.44) occurs for some σ_e because $\frac{c - d}{b + c - a - d}$ is strictly less than one and we obtain

$$
\begin{aligned}
g(1) \ (b - a) &= (\frac{\pi^* - b}{a - b} \ (a - c) + c - \pi^*) \ (b - a) \\
&= (b - \pi^*) \ (a - c) + (c - \pi^*) \ (b - a) \\
&= ab + c\pi^* - ac - b\pi^* \\
&= (a - \pi^*) \ (b - c) \\
&< 0
\end{aligned} \tag{B.55}
$$

which implies that $\pi\left(\frac{\pi^*-d-1\cdot(b-d)}{1\cdot(a+d-b-c)+c-d}, 1\right)$ is strictly less than π^*. Note that

$$\frac{\pi^* - d - 1 \cdot (b - d)}{1 \cdot (a + d - b - c) + c - d} = \frac{\pi^* - b}{a - b} = \frac{b - \pi^*}{b - a} \in (0, 1) \qquad \text{(B.56)}$$

holds since $b > \pi^* > a$. Due to the double null of g at $x = \sigma^*$ and the fact that $\sigma^* > \frac{c-d}{b+c-a-d}$ (see above) we must have

$$\pi\left(\frac{\pi^* - d - \sigma_e(b - d)}{\sigma_e(a + d - b - c) + c - d}, \sigma_e\right) \leq \pi^* \qquad \text{(B.57)}$$

for all $\sigma_e > \frac{c-d}{b+c-a-d}$ such that $\frac{\pi^*-d-\sigma_e(b-d)}{\sigma_e(a+d-b-c)+c-d} \in \Delta$, with equality if and only if $\sigma_e = \sigma^*$.

The first case in (B.44) occurs if and only if $c > d$. If the latter holds true we obtain

$$g(0) = \frac{\pi^* - d}{c - d}(b - d) + d - \pi^*$$

$$= (\pi^* - d)\left(\frac{b - d}{c - d} - 1\right) \qquad \text{(B.58)}$$

$$> (\pi^* - d)(1 - 1)$$

$$= 0.$$

Hence, we must have

$$\pi\left(\frac{\pi^* - d - \sigma_e(b - d)}{\sigma_e(a + d - b - c) + c - d}, \sigma_e\right) > \pi^* \qquad \text{(B.59)}$$

for all $\sigma_e < \frac{c-d}{b+c-a-d}$ such that $\frac{\pi^*-d-\sigma_e(b-d)}{\sigma_e(a+d-b-c)+c-d} \in \Delta$.

Consequently, whenever the entrant generates a fitness of exactly π^*, then an incumbent-type agent's expected fitness is still at least as large as long as $\bar{\sigma}_e < \frac{c-d}{b+c-a-d}$ or $\bar{\sigma}_e = \sigma^*$. However, if $\bar{\sigma}_e > \frac{c-d}{b+c-a-d}$ and $\bar{\sigma}_e \neq \sigma^*$, then the mutant could successfully enter the population provided that $\frac{\pi^*-d-\bar{\sigma}_e(b-d)}{\bar{\sigma}_e(a+d-b-c)+c-d}$ is an element of Δ.

Note that $\frac{\pi^*-d-\sigma_e(b-d)}{\sigma_e(a+d-b-c)+c-d} > 1$ (for $\bar{\sigma}_e < \frac{c-d}{b+c-a-d}$) if and only if $\frac{c-\pi^*}{c-a} < \bar{\sigma}_e < \frac{c-d}{b+c-a-d}$ in case that $c \geq \pi^*$. In case that $c < \pi^*$, this is true for all $\bar{\sigma}_e < \frac{c-d}{b+c-a-d}$. The intuition behind this is clear: If the incumbent-type agent is playing the pure strategy A, then the entrant-type agent's fitness from this match is a convex combination of a and c, which are both strictly less than π^*. Furthermore, we have $\frac{\pi^*-d-\sigma_e(b-d)}{\sigma_e(a+d-b-c)+c-d} < 0$ (for $\bar{\sigma}_e > \frac{c-d}{b+c-a-d}$) if and only if

$\frac{c-d}{b+c-a-d} < \bar{\sigma}_e < \frac{\pi^*-d}{b-d} < 1$ holds. All in all, we obtain the following statement:

i. $c \geq \pi^*$: A population μ is stable w.r.t. π only if its support $C(\mu)$ solely consists of types $T \in \mathcal{T}$ with best-response correspondences that satisfy $\sigma^* \in \beta_T(\sigma^*)$ and for which we have

$$
\beta_T(\sigma_e) \subseteq
\begin{cases}
[0, \frac{\pi^*-d-\sigma_e(b-d)}{\sigma_e(a+d-b-c)+c-d}] & \text{if } 0 \leq \sigma_e \leq \frac{c-\pi^*}{c-a} \\
[0,1] & \text{if } \frac{c-\pi^*}{c-a} < \sigma_e < \frac{\pi^*-d}{b-d} \\
[\sigma^*,1] & \text{if } \sigma_e = \sigma^* \\
(\frac{\pi^*-d-\sigma_e(b-d)}{\sigma_e(a+d-b-c)+c-d},1] & \text{if } \frac{\pi^*-d}{b-d} \leq \sigma_e \leq 1,\ \sigma_e \neq \sigma^*
\end{cases}
\tag{B.60}
$$

ii. $c < \pi^*$: A population μ is stable w.r.t. π only if its support $C(\mu)$ solely consists of types $T \in \mathcal{T}$ with best-response correspondences that satisfy $\sigma^* \in \beta_T(\sigma^*)$ and for which we have

$$
\beta_T(\sigma_e) \subseteq
\begin{cases}
[0,1] & \text{if } 0 \leq \sigma_e < \frac{\pi^*-d}{b-d} \\
[\sigma^*,1] & \text{if } \sigma_e = \sigma^* \\
(\frac{\pi^*-d-\sigma_e(b-d)}{\sigma_e(a+d-b-c)+c-d},1] & \text{if } \frac{\pi^*-d}{b-d} \leq \sigma_e \leq 1,\ \sigma_e \neq \sigma^*
\end{cases}
\tag{B.61}
$$

2nd case: $c > b$. As $b+c > a+d$ and A and B are not efficient we must have $c > \pi^* > a \geq d$. Hence, the first case in (B.44) occurs for some σ_e because $\frac{c-d}{b+c-a-d}$ is strictly positive and we obtain

$$
\begin{aligned}
g(0) &= \frac{\pi^* - d}{c - d}(b - d) + d - \pi^* \\
&= (\pi^* - d)\left(\frac{b - d}{c - d} - 1\right) \\
&< (\pi^* - d)(1 - 1) \\
&= 0.
\end{aligned}
\tag{B.62}
$$

which implies that $\pi(\frac{\pi^*-d-0\cdot(b-d)}{0\cdot(a+d-b-c)+c-d},0)$ is strictly less than π^*. Note that

$$
\frac{\pi^* - d - 0 \cdot (b-d)}{0 \cdot (a+d-b-c) + c - d} = \frac{\pi^* - d}{c - d} \in (0,1)
\tag{B.63}
$$

since $c > \pi^* > d$. Due to the double null of g at $x = \sigma^*$ and the fact that $\sigma^* < \frac{c-d}{b+c-a-d}$ (see above) we must have

$$\pi \left(\frac{\pi^* - d - \sigma_e(b-d)}{\sigma_e(a+d-b-c)+c-d}, \sigma_e\right) \leq \pi^* \qquad (B.64)$$

for all $\sigma_e < \frac{c-d}{b+c-a-d}$ such that $\frac{\pi^*-d-\sigma_e(b-d)}{\sigma_e(a+d-b-c)+c-d} \in \Delta$, with equality if and only if $\sigma_e = \sigma^*$.

The third case in (B.44) occurs if and only if $b > a$. If the latter holds true we obtain

$$\begin{aligned}
g(1)\,(b-a) &= \left(\frac{\pi^* - b}{a-b}\right)(a-c)+c-\pi^*)\,(b-a) \\
&= (b-\pi^*)\,(a-c)+(c-\pi^*)\,(b-a) \\
&= ab + c\pi^* - ac - b\pi^* \qquad (B.65) \\
&= (a-\pi^*)\,(b-c) \\
&> 0.
\end{aligned}$$

Hence, we must have

$$\pi \left(\frac{\pi^* - d - \sigma_e(b-d)}{\sigma_e(a+d-b-c)+c-d}, \sigma_e\right) > \pi^* \qquad (B.66)$$

for all $\sigma_e > \frac{c-d}{b+c-a-d}$ such that $\frac{\pi^*-d-\sigma_e(b-d)}{\sigma_e(a+d-b-c)+c-d} \in [0,1]$.

Consequently, whenever the entrant generates a fitness of exactly π^*, then an incumbent agent's average fitness is still at least as large as long as $\bar{\sigma}_e > \frac{c-d}{b+c-a-d}$ or $\bar{\sigma}_e = \sigma^*$. However, if $\bar{\sigma}_e < \frac{c-d}{b+c-a-d}$ and $\bar{\sigma}_e \neq \sigma^*$, then the mutant could successfully enter the population provided that $\frac{\pi^*-d-\bar{\sigma}_e(b-d)}{\bar{\sigma}_e(a+d-b-c)+c-d} \in \Delta$.

Note that $\frac{\pi^*-d-\sigma_e(b-d)}{\sigma_e(a+d-b-c)+c-d} > 1$ (for $\bar{\sigma}_e < \frac{c-d}{b+c-a-d}$) if and only if $0 < \frac{c-\pi^*}{c-a} < \bar{\sigma}_e < \frac{c-d}{b+c-a-d}$. Furthermore, we have $\frac{\pi^*-d-\sigma_e(b-d)}{\sigma_e(a+d-b-c)+c-d} < 0$ (for $\bar{\sigma}_e > \frac{c-d}{b+c-a-d}$) if and only if $\frac{c-d}{b+c-a-d} < \bar{\sigma}_e < \frac{\pi^*-d}{b-d}$ in case that $b \geq \pi^*$. In case that $b < \pi^*$, this is true for all $\bar{\sigma}_e > \frac{c-d}{b+c-a-d}$. The intuition behind this is clear: If the incumbent-type agent is playing the pure strategy B, then the entrant-type agent's fitness from this match is a convex combination of b and d, which are both strictly less than π^*. All in all, we obtain the following statement:

i. $b \geq \pi^*$: A population μ is stable w.r.t. π only if its support $C(\mu)$ solely consists of types $T \in \mathcal{T}$ with best-response correspondences that satisfy $\sigma^* \in \beta_T(\sigma^*)$ and for which we have

$$\beta_T(\sigma_e) \subseteq \begin{cases} [0, \frac{\pi^*-d-\sigma_e(b-d)}{\sigma_e(a+d-b-c)+c-d}) & \text{if } 0 \le \sigma_e \le \frac{c-\pi^*}{c-a}, \ \sigma_e \neq \sigma^* \\ [0, \sigma^*] & \text{if } \sigma_e = \sigma^* \\ [0, 1] & \text{if } \frac{c-\pi^*}{c-a} < \sigma_e < \frac{\pi^*-d}{b-d} \\ [\frac{\pi^*-d-\sigma_e(b-d)}{\sigma_e(a+d-b-c)+c-d}, 1] & \text{if } \frac{\pi^*-d}{b-d} \le \sigma_e \le 1 \end{cases} \qquad (B.67)$$

ii. $b < \pi^*$: A population μ is stable w.r.t. π only if its support $C(\mu)$ solely consists of types $T \in \mathcal{T}$ with best-response correspondences that satisfy $\sigma^* \in \beta_T(\sigma^*)$ and for which we have

$$\beta_T(\sigma_e) \subseteq \begin{cases} [0, \frac{\pi^*-d-\sigma_e(b-d)}{\sigma_e(a+d-b-c)+c-d}) & \text{if } 0 \le \sigma_e \le \frac{c-\pi^*}{c-a}, \ \sigma_e \neq \sigma^* \\ [0, \sigma^*] & \text{if } \sigma_e = \sigma^* \\ [0, 1] & \text{if } \frac{c-\pi^*}{c-a} < \sigma_e \le 1 \end{cases} \qquad (B.68)$$

□

C

Proofs for Chapter 5

C.1 Proof of Proposition 5.11

Proof. Essentially, the proof of Proposition 2.21 can be directly carried forward to the setup of Chap. 5 with the restricted type space $\mathcal{T_R}$.

In particular, T_0 can be used as a potential entrant where the corresponding agents would outperform the agents of at least some incumbent type of a population in which not all incumbents generate the efficient fitness π^* in all their matches. T_0 belongs to the restricted type space $\mathcal{T_R}$ since agents of this type are indifferent among any two possible strategy profiles. Therefore, this preference relation is obviously continuous and satisfies betweenness in the first component. Conditions *i.* and *ii.* in Definition 5.1 always hold with indifference.

Also, the case when T_0 is an element of $C(\mu_\mathcal{R})$ can be treated using the same substituting preference relation $\succsim_{T_0^\epsilon}$ and utility function $u_{T_0^\epsilon} : \Delta^n \times \Delta^n \to \mathbb{R}$ as defined in (A.10) and (A.11):

$$u_{T_0^\epsilon}(\sigma_T, \sigma_{-T}) \equiv \min\{1, \epsilon^{-1}\|(\sigma_T, \sigma_{-T}) - (e_n, \bar{x})\|_1\}. \qquad (\text{C.1})$$

Here, ϵ is sufficiently small such that for all $\sigma_{-T} \in \Delta_b^n$ and $\sigma_T \in \Delta^n$ we have $u_{T_0^\epsilon}(\sigma_T, \sigma_{-T}) = 1$ and the preference relation $\succsim_{T_0^\epsilon}$ defined by

$$\sigma' \succsim_{T_0^\epsilon} \sigma'' :\Longleftrightarrow u_{T_0^\epsilon}(\sigma') \geq u_{T_0^\epsilon}(\sigma'') \qquad (\text{C.2})$$

is not an element of $C(\mu_\mathcal{R})$.

The only thing left to show is that T_0^ϵ is an element of the restricted type space $\mathcal{T_R}$, i.e. that $\succsim_{T_0^\epsilon}$ is continuous and satisfies betweenness in the first component. Continuity follows immediately from the definition since $u_{T_0^\epsilon}$ is continuous. In order to prove betweenness suppose that $\sigma'_T, \sigma''_T, \bar{\sigma}_{-T} \in \Delta^n$ satisfy $(\sigma'_T, \bar{\sigma}_{-T}) \succsim_{T_0^\epsilon} (\sigma''_T, \bar{\sigma}_{-T})$. Let $\alpha \in [0, 1]$.

1st case: $u_{T_0^\epsilon}(\sigma_T', \bar\sigma_{-T}) = u_{T_0^\epsilon}(\sigma_T'', \bar\sigma_{-T}) = 1$. Then, we have

$$\|(\alpha\,\sigma_T' + (1-\alpha)\,\sigma_T'', \bar\sigma_{-T}) - (e_n, \bar x)\|_1$$

$$= 2\sum_{i=1}^{n-1}(\alpha\,\sigma_T'^i + (1-\alpha)\sigma_T''^i) + \|\bar\sigma_{-T} - \bar x\|_1$$

$$= \alpha\left(2\sum_{i=1}^{n-1}\sigma_T'^i + \|\bar\sigma_{-T} - \bar x\|_1\right)$$

$$\qquad + (1-\alpha)\left(2\sum_{i=1}^{n-1}\sigma_T''^i + \|\bar\sigma_{-T} - \bar x\|_1\right) \tag{C.3}$$

$$= \alpha\,\|(\sigma_T', \bar\sigma_{-T}) - (e_n, \bar x)\|_1$$

$$\qquad + (1-\alpha)\,\|(\sigma_T'', \bar\sigma_{-T}) - (e_n, \bar x)\|_1$$

$$\geq \alpha\,\epsilon + (1-\alpha)\,\epsilon = \epsilon.$$

Therefore, we have $u_{T_0^\epsilon}(\alpha\,\sigma_T' + (1-\alpha)\,\sigma_T'', \bar\sigma_{-T}) = 1$ and thus

$$(\sigma_T', \bar\sigma_{-T}) \;\sim_{T_0^\epsilon}\; (\alpha\,\sigma_T' + (1-\alpha)\,\sigma_T'', \bar\sigma_{-T}) \tag{C.4}$$

and

$$(\alpha\,\sigma_T' + (1-\alpha)\,\sigma_T'', \bar\sigma_{-T}) \;\sim_{T_0^\epsilon}\; (\sigma_T'', \bar\sigma_{-T}). \tag{C.5}$$

2nd case: $u_{T_0^\epsilon}(\sigma_T'', \bar\sigma_{-T}) = b \leq a = u_{T_0^\epsilon}(\sigma_T', \bar\sigma_{-T}) < 1$ for some $a, b \in [0, 1)$. Then, we have

$$\|(\alpha\,\sigma_T' + (1-\alpha)\,\sigma_T'', \bar\sigma_{-T}) - (e_n, \bar x)\|_1$$

$$= 2\sum_{i=1}^{n-1}(\alpha\,\sigma_T'^i + (1-\alpha)\sigma_T''^i) + \|\bar\sigma_{-T} - \bar x\|_1$$

$$= \alpha\left(2\sum_{i=1}^{n-1}\sigma_T'^i + \|\bar\sigma_{-T} - \bar x\|_1\right)$$

$$\qquad + (1-\alpha)\left(2\sum_{i=1}^{n-1}\sigma_T''^i + \|\bar\sigma_{-T} - \bar x\|_1\right) \tag{C.6}$$

$$= \alpha\,\|(\sigma_T', \bar\sigma_{-T}) - (e_n, \bar x)\|_1$$

$$\qquad + (1-\alpha)\,\|(\sigma_T'', \bar\sigma_{-T}) - (e_n, \bar x)\|_1$$

$$= \alpha\,a\,\epsilon + (1-\alpha)\,b\,\epsilon \;\in\; [b\,\epsilon, a\,\epsilon].$$

Therefore, we have $u_{T_0^\epsilon}(\alpha\,\sigma'_T + (1-\alpha)\,\sigma''_T, \bar\sigma_{-T}) \in [b, a]$ and thus

$$(\sigma'_T, \bar\sigma_{-T}) \succsim_{T_0^\epsilon} (\alpha\,\sigma'_T + (1-\alpha)\,\sigma''_T, \bar\sigma_{-T}) \tag{C.7}$$

and

$$(\alpha\,\sigma'_T + (1-\alpha)\,\sigma''_T, \bar\sigma_{-T}) \succsim_{T_0^\epsilon} (\sigma''_T, \bar\sigma_{-T}). \tag{C.8}$$

3rd case: $u_{T_0^\epsilon}(\sigma''_T, \bar\sigma_{-T}) = c < 1 = u_{T_0^\epsilon}(\sigma'_T, \bar\sigma_{-T})$ for some $c \in [0, 1)$.
Then, we have

$$
\begin{aligned}
\|(\alpha\,&\sigma'_T + (1-\alpha)\,\sigma''_T, \bar\sigma_{-T}) - (e_n, \bar x)\|_1 \\
&= 2\sum_{i=1}^{n-1}(\alpha\,\sigma'^i_T + (1-\alpha)\sigma''^i_T) + \|\bar\sigma_{-T} - \bar x\|_1 \\
&= \alpha\,\Big(2\sum_{i=1}^{n-1}\sigma'^i_T + \|\bar\sigma_{-T} - \bar x\|_1\Big) \\
&\quad + (1-\alpha)\Big(2\sum_{i=1}^{n-1}\sigma''^i_T + \|\bar\sigma_{-T} - \bar x\|_1\Big) \\
&= \alpha\,\|(\sigma'_T, \bar\sigma_{-T}) - (e_n, \bar x)\|_1 \\
&\quad + (1-\alpha)\,\|(\sigma''_T, \bar\sigma_{-T}) - (e_n, \bar x)\|_1 \\
&\geq \alpha\,\epsilon + (1-\alpha)\,c\,\epsilon \;\geq\; c\,\epsilon.
\end{aligned}
\tag{C.9}
$$

Therefore, we have $u_{T_0^\epsilon}(\alpha\,\sigma'_T + (1-\alpha)\,\sigma''_T, \bar\sigma_{-T}) \in [c, 1]$ and thus

$$(\sigma'_T, \bar\sigma_{-T}) \succsim_{T_0^\epsilon} (\alpha\,\sigma'_T + (1-\alpha)\,\sigma''_T, \bar\sigma_{-T}) \tag{C.10}$$

and

$$(\alpha\,\sigma'_T + (1-\alpha)\,\sigma''_T, \bar\sigma_{-T}) \succsim_{T_0^\epsilon} (\sigma''_T, \bar\sigma_{-T}). \tag{C.11}$$

The special characteristic of a mutant we have just constructed, T_0 or an appropriate T_0^ϵ, is as in the proof of Proposition 2.21. Agents of such a type can imitate any incumbent's behavior. For, in any match with an opponent of a type from the population μ which plays according to the equilibrium configuration function b, the mutant-type agent is indifferent among all possible strategies and can thus mimic the play of the particular incumbent-type agent that is most successful in terms of the fitness values against the given opponent.

The rest of the proof is exactly as shown in Proposition 2.21.   □

C.2 Proof of Theorem 5.12

Proof. Consider a monomorphic population in which the only type T_{a_i} induces a best-response correspondence $\beta_{T_{a_i}}$ as follows:

$$\beta_{T_i}(\sigma) = \{a_i\} \quad \forall\, \sigma \in \Delta^n \tag{C.12}$$

The pure strategy a_i is a dominant strategy for agents of this type. T_{a_i} is well-defined since a preference relation in $\mathcal{T}_{\mathcal{R}}$ inducing the best-response correspondence defined in (C.12) in fact exists. Take, for instance, a preference relation $\succsim_{T_{a_i}}$ which is represented by the utility function $u_{T_{a_i}} : \Delta^n \times \Delta^n \to \mathbb{R}$ defined by

$$u_{T_{a_i}}(\sigma_T, \sigma_{-T}) = \sigma_T^i. \tag{C.13}$$

This preference relation is continuous since $u_{T_{a_i}}$ is continuous. In order to see that it also satisfies betweenness in the first component suppose that the strategies $\sigma_T', \sigma_T'', \bar{\sigma}_{-T} \in \Delta^n$ are such that $(\sigma_T', \bar{\sigma}_{-T}) \succsim_{T_{a_i}} (\sigma_T'', \bar{\sigma}_{-T})$ holds. Further, let $\alpha \in [0,1]$. By assumption, we have $u_{T_{a_i}}(\sigma_T', \bar{\sigma}_{-T}) \geq u_{T_{a_i}}(\sigma_T'', \bar{\sigma}_{-T})$ which is equivalent to $\sigma_T'^i \geq \sigma_T''^i$. The latter implies that

$$u_{T_{a_i}}(\alpha\, \sigma_T' + (1-\alpha)\, \sigma_T'', \bar{\sigma}_{-T}) = \alpha\, \sigma_T'^i + (1-\alpha)\, \sigma_T''^i \in [\sigma_T''^i, \sigma_T'^i] \tag{C.14}$$

holds. Therefore, we have

$$(\sigma_T', \bar{\sigma}_{-T}) \succsim_{T_{a_i}} (\alpha\, \sigma_T' + (1-\alpha)\, \sigma_T'', \bar{\sigma}_{-T}) \tag{C.15}$$

and

$$(\alpha\, \sigma_T' + (1-\alpha)\, \sigma_T'', \bar{\sigma}_{-T}) \succsim_{T_{a_i}} (\sigma_T'', \bar{\sigma}_{-T}). \tag{C.16}$$

Consider the unique equilibrium configuration $b_{T_{a_i}}(T_{a_i}) = a_i$. We claim that a_i is stable w.r.t. the fitness function π, with this monomorphic population. Let an entrant type, say T_e, into the population be such that in the post-entry equilibrium configuration $\bar{b}$ the Nash equilibrium which is played between an entrant-type agent and an incumbent-type agent is $(\sigma_e, \sigma_i) \equiv (\bar{b}_{T_e}(T_{a_i}), \bar{b}_{T_{a_i}}(T_e))$ and the Nash equilibrium between two entrant-type agents is $(\sigma_3, \sigma_3) \equiv (\bar{b}_{T_e}(T_e), \bar{b}_{T_e}(T_e))$. The average fitness generated by the incumbent and the entrant are, respectively, given by

$$\Pi_{T_{a_i}}((1-\epsilon)\, \delta_{T_{a_i}} + \epsilon\, \delta_{T_e} \mid \bar{b}) = (1-\epsilon)\, \pi^* + \epsilon\, \pi(a_i, \sigma_e) \tag{C.17}$$

and

$$\Pi_{T_e}((1-\epsilon)\,\delta_{T_{a_i}} + \epsilon\,\delta_{T_e} \mid \bar{b}) = (1-\epsilon)\,\pi(\sigma_e, a_i) + \epsilon\,\pi(\sigma_3, \sigma_3). \quad \text{(C.18)}$$

If $\sigma_e \neq a_i$, then we have by assumption that

$$\pi(\sigma_e, a_i) = \sum_{j=1}^{n} \sigma_e^j\,\pi(a_j, a_i) < \pi(a_i, a_i). \quad \text{(C.19)}$$

Hence, for sufficiently small $\epsilon > 0$ we have $\Pi_{T_{a_i}}(.) > \Pi_{T_e}(.)$. If $\sigma_e = a_i$, then we have

$$\pi(a_i, \sigma_e) = \pi(a_i, a_i) \geq \pi(\sigma_3, \sigma_3) \quad \text{(C.20)}$$

since a_i is efficient. We obtain that $\Pi_{T_{a_i}}(.) \geq \Pi_{T_e}(.)$ holds regardless of the size of ϵ. The average fitness generated by the entrant never exceeds that of the incumbent.

We refrain from proving existence of a uniform invasion barrier $\epsilon > 0$ that would work for all types in $\mathcal{T}_\mathcal{R}$ and all post-entry equilibrium configurations. Such evidence is provided in the proof of Proposition 1 in [14] and the arguments can be taken over here. Also note that the second part of our proof above is in essence the same as the one in the cited work. We have that $(\delta_{T_{a_i}}, b)$ is stable w.r.t. π.   □

C.3 Proof of Lemma 5.13

Proof. The proof of Proposition 3a in [14] can be directly brought forward to our setup. However, we still need to show that the preference relation used is an element of our restricted type space $\mathcal{T}_\mathcal{R}$.

1st case: $a > c$. We have

$$\pi(A, A) = a > c = \pi(B, A). \quad \text{(C.21)}$$

The claim follows immediately from Theorem 5.12.

2nd case: $c \geq a$. Consider a monomorphic population in which the only type T_i induces a best-response correspondence β_{T_i} as follows:

$$\beta_{T_i}(\sigma) = \begin{cases} [0,1] & \text{if } \sigma = 1 \\ \{0\} & \text{otherwise} \end{cases}. \quad \text{(C.22)}$$

The pure strategy B is a weakly dominant strategy for agents of this type. Such an agent randomizes only if its opponent plays A with probability one. T_i is well-defined since a preference relation in $\mathcal{T}_\mathcal{R}$ inducing the best-response correspondence defined in (C.22) in fact exists. Take, for instance, a preference relation $\succsim_{T_i}$ which is represented by the utility function $u_{T_i} : \Delta \times \Delta \to \mathbb{R}$ defined by

$$u_{T_i}(\sigma_T, \sigma_{-T}) = (1 - \sigma_T)\,(1 - \sigma_{-T}). \qquad (\text{C.23})$$

This preference relation is continuous since u_{T_i} is continuous. In order to see that it also satisfies betweenness in the first component suppose that the strategies $\sigma'_T, \sigma''_T, \bar{\sigma}_{-T} \in \Delta$ are such that $(\sigma'_T, \bar{\sigma}_{-T}) \succsim_{T_i} (\sigma''_T, \bar{\sigma}_{-T})$ holds. Further, let $\alpha \in [0, 1]$. By assumption, we have $u_{T_i}(\sigma'_T, \bar{\sigma}_{-T}) \geq u_{T_i}(\sigma''_T, \bar{\sigma}_{-T})$ which is equivalent to

$$(1 - \sigma'_T)\,(1 - \bar{\sigma}_{-T}) \geq (1 - \sigma''_T)\,(1 - \bar{\sigma}_{-T}). \qquad (\text{C.24})$$

Obviously, we have

$$\begin{aligned}
&(1 - \sigma'_T)\,(1 - \bar{\sigma}_{-T}) \\
&\quad \geq (1 - (\alpha\,\sigma'_T + (1 - \alpha)\,\sigma''_T))\,(1 - \bar{\sigma}_{-T}) \qquad (\text{C.25}) \\
&\quad \geq (1 - \sigma''_T)\,(1 - \bar{\sigma}_{-T})
\end{aligned}$$

Therefore, we have

$$(\sigma'_T, \bar{\sigma}_{-T}) \succsim_{T_i} (\alpha\,\sigma'_T + (1 - \alpha)\,\sigma''_T, \bar{\sigma}_{-T}) \qquad (\text{C.26})$$

and

$$(\alpha\,\sigma'_T + (1 - \alpha)\,\sigma''_T, \bar{\sigma}_{-T}) \succsim_{T_i} (\sigma''_T, \bar{\sigma}_{-T}). \qquad (\text{C.27})$$

Now, consider the equilibrium configuration in which $b_{T_i}(T_i) = 1$, i.e. where all agents play the pure strategy A in all their interactions. We claim that this monomorphic population together with b is stable w.r.t. the fitness function π. Let an entrant type, say T_e, into the population be such that in the post-entry equilibrium configuration $\bar{b}$ the Nash equilibrium which is played between an entrant-type agent and an incumbent-type agent is $(\sigma_e, \sigma_i) \equiv (\bar{b}_{T_e}(T_i), \bar{b}_{T_i}(T_e))$ and the Nash equilibrium between two entrant-type agents is $(\sigma_3, \sigma_3) \equiv (\bar{b}_{T_e}(T_e), \bar{b}_{T_e}(T_e))$. The average fitness generated by the incumbent and the entrant are, respectively, given by

$$\Pi_{T_i}((1 - \epsilon)\,\delta_{T_i} + \epsilon\,\delta_{T_e} \mid \bar{b}) = (1 - \epsilon)\,a + \epsilon\,\pi(\sigma_i, \sigma_e) \qquad (\text{C.28})$$

and

$$\Pi_{T_e}((1 - \epsilon)\,\delta_{T_i} + \epsilon\,\delta_{T_e} \mid \bar{b}) = (1 - \epsilon)\,\pi(\sigma_e, \sigma_i) + \epsilon\,\pi(\sigma_3, \sigma_3). \qquad (\text{C.29})$$

If $\sigma_e = 1$, then $c \geq a \geq b$ and $\pi(\sigma_3, \sigma_3) \leq \pi^* = a$ imply that

$$\Pi_{T_i}((1 - \epsilon)\,\delta_{T_i} + \epsilon\,\delta_{T_e} \mid \bar{b})$$

$$= (1 - \epsilon)\,a + \epsilon\,(\sigma_i\,a + (1 - \sigma_i)\,c)$$

$$\geq a \tag{C.30}$$

$$\geq (1 - \epsilon)\,(\sigma_i\,a + (1 - \sigma_i)\,b) + \epsilon\,\pi(\sigma_3, \sigma_3)$$

$$= \Pi_{T_e}((1 - \epsilon)\,\delta_{T_i} + \epsilon\,\delta_{T_e} \mid \bar{b})$$

holds independently of the size of ϵ. If $\sigma_e \neq 1$, then we must have $\sigma_i = 0$ and

$$\Pi_{T_i}((1 - \epsilon)\,\delta_{T_i} + \epsilon\,\delta_{T_e} \mid \bar{b}) - \Pi_{T_e}((1 - \epsilon)\,\delta_{T_i} + \epsilon\,\delta_{T_e} \mid \bar{b})$$

$$= (1 - \epsilon)\,(a - (\sigma_e\,b + (1 - \sigma_e)\,d))$$

$$+ \epsilon\,(\sigma_e\,c + (1 - \sigma_e)\,d - \pi(\sigma_3, \sigma_3))$$

$$\geq (1 - \epsilon)\,(a - (\sigma_e\,b + (1 - \sigma_e)\,d)) \tag{C.31}$$

$$+ \epsilon\,(\sigma_e\,b + (1 - \sigma_e)\,d - a)$$

$$= (1 - 2\epsilon)\,(a - (\sigma_e\,b + (1 - \sigma_e)\,d)).$$

From this it follows that $\Pi_{T_i}(\cdot) \geq \Pi_{T_e}(\cdot)$ if $\epsilon \in (0, \frac{1}{2})$ holds.

Therefore, for any $T_e \notin C(\delta_{T_i})$, $\epsilon \in (0, \frac{1}{2})$ and $\bar{b} \in B((1-\epsilon)\,\delta_{T_i} + \epsilon\,\delta_{T_e})$ the average fitness generated by an entrant T_e can never exceed that of the incumbent type T_i since the former enters in sufficiently small proportion. □

C.4 Proof of Lemma 5.14

Proof. We consider several possible cases with pairs of monomorphic populations and equilibrium configurations such that the strategy profile (σ^*, σ^*) is played in all matches according to the respective population.

Define the function $f : [0, 1] \to \mathbb{R}$ by

$$f(\sigma) = \sigma^2\,a + \sigma\,(1 - \sigma)\,(b + c) + (1 - \sigma)^2\,d\,-a. \tag{C.32}$$

Since A and σ^* are efficient w.r.t. π, we have

$$f(1) = 0 = f(\sigma^*) \tag{C.33}$$

and $f \leq 0$. Rewriting f leads to

$$f(\sigma) = (a + d - b - c)\,\sigma^2 + (b + c - 2d)\,\sigma + d - a. \qquad (C.34)$$

If $\sigma^* = 0$, then we must have $a = d$. In this case both pure strategies, A and B, are efficient. By renaming these two pure strategies the claim follows directly from Lemma 5.13. Hence, we will concentrate our attention to the case in which $\sigma^* \in (0,1)$ holds. Then, 1 and σ^* can both maximize f only if $f = 0$, in which case all strategies $\sigma \in [0,1]$ are efficient. Consequently, we have $a = d$ and $b + c = 2a$.

1st case: $a = d = b$. We must have $b + c = 2d$ which implies that

$$a = b = c = d = \pi^*. \qquad (C.35)$$

The strategy σ^* is trivially stable w.r.t. π^*, for instance with a monomorphic population in which the only type is $T_0 \in \mathcal{T_R}$ and where the equilibrium configuration is $b_{T_0}(T_0) = \sigma^*$. For, the fitness generated for any agent is equal to π^* from all matches. Obviously, no type can ever yield a strictly higher fitness than any other type. Note that in this case all strategies are stable w.r.t. π^*.

2nd case: $a = d > b$. We have $c = 2a - b > a$. Consider a monomorphic population in which the only type T_{0,σ^*} induces a best-response correspondence $\beta_{T_{0,\sigma^*}}$ as follows:

$$\beta_{T_{0,\sigma^*}}(\sigma) = \begin{cases} [0,\ \sigma^*] & \text{if } \sigma = \sigma^* \\ \{0\} & \text{otherwise} \end{cases}. \qquad (C.36)$$

The pure strategy B is a weakly dominant strategy for agents of this type. Such an agent randomizes only if its opponent chooses the strategy $\sigma^* \in \Delta$. The type T_{0,σ^*} is well-defined since a preference relation in $\mathcal{T_R}$ inducing the best-response correspondence defined in (C.36) in fact exists. Take, for instance, a preference relation $\succsim_{T_{0,\sigma^*}}$ which is represented by the utility function $u_{T_{0,\sigma^*}} : \Delta \times \Delta \to \mathbb{R}$ defined by

$$u_{T_{0,\sigma^*}}(\sigma_T, \sigma_{-T}) = (1 - \sigma_T)\,|\sigma_{-T} - \sigma^*| - \max\{0, \sigma_T - \sigma^*\}. \qquad (C.37)$$

This preference relation is continuous since $u_{T_{0,\sigma^*}}$ is continuous. It also satisfies betweenness in the first component because for any $\bar{\sigma}_{-T} \in \Delta$ we have that $u_{T_{0,\sigma^*}}(\,\cdot\,, \bar{\sigma}_{-T})$ is monotonically decreasing.

Now, consider the equilibrium configuration in which $b_{T_{0,\sigma^*}}(T_{0,\sigma^*}) = \sigma^*$, i.e. where all agents play the strategy σ^* in all their interactions. We claim that this monomorphic population together with b is stable w.r.t. the fitness function π. Let an entrant type, say T_e, into the population be such that in the post-entry equilibrium configuration $\bar{b}$ the Nash equilibrium which is played between an entrant-type agent and an incumbent-type agent is $(\sigma_e, \sigma_i) \equiv (\bar{b}_{T_e}(T_{0,\sigma^*}), \bar{b}_{T_{0,\sigma^*}}(T_e))$ and the Nash equilibrium between two entrant-type agents is $(\sigma_3, \sigma_3) \equiv (\bar{b}_{T_e}(T_e), \bar{b}_{T_e}(T_e))$. The average fitness generated by the incumbent and the entrant are, respectively, given by

$$\Pi_{T_{0,\sigma^*}}((1-\epsilon)\,\delta_{T_{0,\sigma^*}} + \epsilon\,\delta_{T_e} \mid \bar{b}) = (1-\epsilon)\,\pi^* + \epsilon\,\pi(\sigma_i, \sigma_e) \quad \text{(C.38)}$$

and

$$\Pi_{T_e}((1-\epsilon)\,\delta_{T_{0,\sigma^*}} + \epsilon\,\delta_{T_e} \mid \bar{b})$$
$$= (1-\epsilon)\,\pi(\sigma_e, \sigma_i) + \epsilon\,\pi(\sigma_3, \sigma_3). \quad \text{(C.39)}$$

If $\sigma_e \neq \sigma^*$, then $\sigma_i = 0$. We have

$$\Pi_{T_{0,\sigma^*}}((1-\epsilon)\,\delta_{T_{0,\sigma^*}} + \epsilon\,\delta_{T_e} \mid \bar{b})$$
$$= (1-\epsilon)\,\pi^* + \epsilon\,(\sigma_e\,c + (1-\sigma_e)\,d)$$
$$\geq \pi^* \quad \text{(C.40)}$$
$$\geq (1-\epsilon)\,(\sigma_e\,b + (1-\sigma_e)\,d) + \epsilon\,\pi(\sigma_3, \sigma_3)$$
$$= \Pi_{T_e}((1-\epsilon)\,\delta_{T_{0,\sigma^*}} + \epsilon\,\delta_{T_e} \mid \bar{b}),$$

independently of the size of ϵ. If $\sigma_e = \sigma^*$, then we have

$$\pi(\sigma_e, \sigma_i) = \sigma_i\,[\sigma^* a + (1-\sigma^*)c]$$
$$+ (1-\sigma_i)\,[\sigma^* b + (1-\sigma^*)d] \quad \text{(C.41)}$$
$$\leq \pi^*$$

and

$$\pi(\sigma_i, \sigma_e) = \sigma_i\,[\sigma^* a + (1-\sigma^*)b]$$
$$+ (1-\sigma_i)\,[\sigma^* c + (1-\sigma^*)d] \quad \text{(C.42)}$$
$$\geq \pi^*$$

for any $\sigma_i \in [0, \sigma^*]$ (with equalities for $\sigma_i = \sigma^*$). From this it follows that $\Pi_{T_{0,\sigma^*}}(\cdot) \geq \Pi_{T_e}(\cdot)$ holds independently of the size of ϵ. The average fitness generated by the entrant never exceeds that of the incumbent.

3rd case: $b > a = d$. We have $c = 2a - b < a$. Consider a monomorphic population in which the only type T_{1,σ^*} induces a best-response correspondence $\beta_{T_{1,\sigma^*}}$ as follows:

$$\beta_{T_{1,\sigma*}}(\sigma) = \begin{cases} [\sigma^*, 1] & \text{if } \sigma = \sigma^* \\ \{1\} & \text{otherwise} \end{cases}. \qquad (C.43)$$

The pure strategy A is a weakly dominant strategy for agents of this type. Such an agent randomizes only if its opponent chooses the strategy $\sigma^* \in \Delta$. The type $T_{1,\sigma*}$ is well-defined since a preference relation in $\mathcal{T}_{\mathcal{R}}$ inducing the best-response correspondence defined in (C.43) in fact exists. Take, for instance, a preference relation $\succsim_{T_{1,\sigma*}}$ which is represented by the utility function $u_{T_{1,\sigma*}} : \Delta \times \Delta \to \mathbb{R}$ defined by

$$u_{T_{1,\sigma*}}(\sigma_T, \sigma_{-T}) = \sigma_T \,|\sigma_{-T} - \sigma^*| + \min\{0, \sigma_T - \sigma^*\}. \qquad (C.44)$$

This preference relation is continuous since $u_{T_{0,\sigma*}}$ is continuous. It also satisfies betweenness in the first component because for any $\bar{\sigma}_{-T} \in \Delta$ we have that $u_{T_{0,\sigma*}}(\,\cdot\,, \bar{\sigma}_{-T})$ is monotonically increasing.

Now, consider the equilibrium configuration in which $b_{T_{1,\sigma*}}(T_{1,\sigma*}) = \sigma^*$, i.e. where all agents play the strategy σ^* in all their interactions. We claim that this monomorphic population together with b is stable w.r.t. the fitness function π. Let an entrant type, say T_e, into the population be such that in the post-entry equilibrium configuration $\bar{b}$ the Nash equilibrium which is played between an entrant-type agent and an incumbent-type agent is $(\sigma_e, \sigma_i) \equiv (\bar{b}_{T_e}(T_{1,\sigma*}), \bar{b}_{T_{1,\sigma*}}(T_e))$ and the Nash equilibrium between two entrant-type agents is $(\sigma_3, \sigma_3) \equiv (\bar{b}_{T_e}(T_e), \bar{b}_{T_e}(T_e))$. The average fitness generated by the incumbent and the entrant are, respectively, given by

$$\Pi_{T_{1,\sigma*}}((1 - \epsilon)\, \delta_{T_{1,\sigma*}} + \epsilon\, \delta_{T_e} \mid \bar{b}) = (1 - \epsilon)\, \pi^* + \epsilon\, \pi(\sigma_i, \sigma_e) \qquad (C.45)$$

and

$$\begin{aligned} \Pi_{T_e}((1 - \epsilon)\, \delta_{T_{1,\sigma*}} + \epsilon\, \delta_{T_e} \mid \bar{b}) \\ = (1 - \epsilon)\, \pi(\sigma_e, \sigma_i) + \epsilon\, \pi(\sigma_3, \sigma_3). \end{aligned} \qquad (C.46)$$

If $\sigma_e \neq \sigma^*$, then $\sigma_i = 1$. We have

$$\begin{aligned} \Pi_{T_{1,\sigma*}}((1 - \epsilon)\, \delta_{T_{1,\sigma*}} + \epsilon\, \delta_{T_e} \mid \bar{b}) \\ = (1 - \epsilon)\, \pi^* + \epsilon\, (\sigma_e\, a + (1 - \sigma_e)\, b) \\ \geq \pi^* \\ \geq (1 - \epsilon)\, (\sigma_e\, a + (1 - \sigma_e)\, c) + \epsilon\, \pi(\sigma_3, \sigma_3) \\ = \Pi_{T_e}((1 - \epsilon)\, \delta_{T_{1,\sigma*}} + \epsilon\, \delta_{T_e} \mid \bar{b}), \end{aligned} \qquad (C.47)$$

independently of the size of ϵ. If $\sigma_e = \sigma^*$, then we have

$$\pi(\sigma_e, \sigma_i) = \sigma_i \left[\sigma^* a + (1 - \sigma^*) c \right]$$
$$+ (1 - \sigma_i) \left[\sigma^* b + (1 - \sigma^*) d \right] \qquad (C.48)$$
$$\leq \pi^*$$

and

$$\pi(\sigma_i, \sigma_e) = \sigma_i \left[\sigma^* a + (1 - \sigma^*) b \right]$$
$$+ (1 - \sigma_i) \left[\sigma^* c + (1 - \sigma^*) d \right] \qquad (C.49)$$
$$\geq \pi^*$$

for any $\sigma_i \in [0, \sigma^*]$ (with equalities for $\sigma_i = \sigma^*$). From this it follows that $\Pi_{T_1, \sigma^*}(\cdot) \geq \Pi_{T_e}(\cdot)$ holds independently of the size of ϵ. The average fitness generated by the entrant never exceeds that of the incumbent.

□

C.5 Proof of Lemma 5.16

Proof. Since A is not efficient w.r.t. π, the other pure strategy, B, cannot be efficient w.r.t. π either because we have assumed that $a \geq d$. Hence, $\sigma^* \in (0, 1)$ must hold. By definition, we have

$$\{\sigma^*\} = \underset{\sigma \in [0,1]}{\mathrm{argmax}} \ \sigma^2 \, a + \sigma \, (1 - \sigma) \, (b + c) + (1 - \sigma)^2 \, d, \qquad (C.50)$$

which yields

$$\sigma^* = \frac{b + c - 2d}{2 \, (b + c - a - d)} \qquad (C.51)$$

via the first-order condition. The efficient fitness is

$$\pi^* \equiv \pi(\sigma^*, \sigma^*)$$
$$= (\sigma^*)^2 \, a + \sigma^* (1 - \sigma^*) \, (b + c) + (1 - \sigma^*)^2 \, d \qquad (C.52)$$
$$= d + \frac{(b + c - 2d)^2}{4 \, (b + c - a - d)}.$$

The non-efficiency of A and B implies that we have $\pi^* > a \geq d$.

In the following, we consider pairs of monomorphic populations and equilibrium configurations. In each case, σ^* is assumed to be played in any match within the respective population. We show that in each such case no mutant type can successfully invade the respective population.

1st case: $b > c \geq \pi^*$. Define $\bar{\sigma}$ such that $\pi^* = \bar{\sigma}\, a + (1 - \bar{\sigma})\, c$ holds, i.e. we have

$$\bar{\sigma} = \frac{c - \pi^*}{c - a}. \tag{C.53}$$

First, we investigate the algebraic sign of $\bar{\sigma} - \sigma^*$. By (C.52), we have

$$4\,(c - a)(b + c - a - d)(\bar{\sigma} - \sigma^*)$$

$$= 4\,(c - a)(b + c - a - d)\left(\frac{c - \pi^*}{c - a} - \frac{b + c - 2d}{2\,(b + c - a - d)}\right)$$

$$= 4\,(b + c - a - d)(c - \pi^*) - 2\,(b + c - 2d)(c - a) \tag{C.54}$$

$$= 4\,(c - d)(b + c - a - d)$$

$$\quad - (b + c - 2d)^2 - 2\,(b + c - 2d)(c - a)$$

$$= (c - b)(b + c - 2a).$$

As we have $c > a$, $b + c > a + d$ and $b + c > 2a$ it follows that $\bar{\sigma} > \sigma^*$ if $c > b$ (this fact will be used in subsequent cases) and $\bar{\sigma} < \sigma^*$ if $b > c$.

Further, define $\bar{\bar{\sigma}}$ such that $\pi^* = \bar{\bar{\sigma}}\, b + (1 - \bar{\bar{\sigma}})\, d$, i.e. we have

$$\bar{\bar{\sigma}} = \frac{\pi^* - d}{b - d}. \tag{C.55}$$

Again, we investigate the algebraic sign of $\bar{\bar{\sigma}} - \bar{\sigma}$ and by (C.52) we have that

$$(c - a)(b - d)(\bar{\bar{\sigma}} - \bar{\sigma}) = (\pi^* - d)(c - a) - (c - \pi^*)(b - d)$$

$$= \frac{1}{4}(b - c)^2 > 0 \tag{C.56}$$

holds. As $c > a$ and $b > d$, we conclude that $\bar{\bar{\sigma}} > \bar{\sigma}$.

Consider a monomorphic population in which the only type T' induces a best-response correspondence $\beta_{T'}$ as follows:

$$\beta_{T'}(\sigma) = \begin{cases} \{1\} & \text{if } \sigma > \bar{\sigma} \text{ and } \sigma \neq \sigma^* \\ [\sigma^*, 1] & \text{if } \sigma = \sigma^* \\ [0, 1] & \text{if } \sigma = \bar{\sigma} \\ \{0\} & \text{if } \sigma < \bar{\sigma} \end{cases} \tag{C.57}$$

The type T' is well-defined since a preference relation in $\mathcal{T}_R$ inducing the best-response correspondence defined in (C.57) in fact exists. Take, for instance, a preference relation $\succsim_{T'}$ which is represented by the utility function $u_{T'} : \Delta \times \Delta \to \mathbb{R}$ defined by

$$u_{T'}(\sigma_T, \sigma_{-T}) = (\sigma_{-T} - \bar{\sigma})\,(\sigma_T\,|\sigma_{-T} - \sigma^*| + \min\{\sigma_T - \sigma^*, 0\}). \quad \text{(C.58)}$$

This preference relation is continuous since $u_{T'}$ is continuous. It also satisfies betweenness in the first component because for any $\bar{\sigma}_{-T} \in \Delta$ we have that $u_{T'}(\,\cdot\,,\bar{\sigma}_{-T})$ is a monotone (i.e. increasing or decreasing) function.

Now, consider the equilibrium configuration b in which $b_{T'}(T') = \sigma^*$, i.e. where all agents play the strategy σ^* in all their interactions. We claim that this monomorphic population together with b is stable w.r.t. the fitness function π. Let an entrant type, say T_e, into the population be such that in the post-entry equilibrium configuration $\bar{b}$ the Nash equilibrium which is played between an entrant-type agent and an incumbent-type agent is $(\sigma_e, \sigma_i) \equiv (\bar{b}_{T_e}(T'), \bar{b}_{T'}(T_e))$ and the Nash equilibrium between two entrant-type agents is $(\sigma_3, \sigma_3) \equiv (\bar{b}_{T_e}(T_e), \bar{b}_{T_e}(T_e))$. The average fitness generated by the incumbent and the entrant are, respectively, given by

$$\Pi_{T'}((1 - \epsilon)\,\delta_{T'} + \epsilon\,\delta_{T_e} \mid \bar{b}) = (1 - \epsilon)\,\pi^* + \epsilon\,\pi(\sigma_i, \sigma_e) \quad \text{(C.59)}$$

and

$$\Pi_{T_e}((1 - \epsilon)\,\delta_{T'} + \epsilon\,\delta_{T_e} \mid \bar{b}) = (1 - \epsilon)\,\pi(\sigma_e, \sigma_i) + \epsilon\,\pi(\sigma_3, \sigma_3). \quad \text{(C.60)}$$

$i.$ If $\sigma_e < \bar{\sigma}$, then $\sigma_i = 0$. We have

$$\begin{aligned}
\Pi_{T'}(&(1 - \epsilon)\,\delta_{T'} + \epsilon\,\delta_{T_e} \mid \bar{b}) - \Pi_{T_e}((1 - \epsilon)\,\delta_{T'} + \epsilon\,\delta_{T_e} \mid \bar{b}) \\
&= (1 - \epsilon)\,(\pi^* - (\sigma_e\,b + (1 - \sigma_e)\,d)) \\
&\quad + \epsilon\,(\sigma_e\,c + (1 - \sigma_e)\,d - \pi(\sigma_3, \sigma_3)) \\
&> (1 - \epsilon)\,(\pi^* - (\bar{\sigma}\,b + (1 - \bar{\sigma})\,d)) + \epsilon\,(d - \pi^*),
\end{aligned} \quad \text{(C.61)}$$

where the latter expression is positive for any $\epsilon \in (0, \frac{\pi^* - (\bar{\sigma}b + (1 - \bar{\sigma})d)}{2\pi^* - (\bar{\sigma}b + (1 - \bar{\sigma})d) - d})$ because

$$\underline{\sigma}\,b + (1 - \underline{\sigma})\,d \;<\; \bar{\sigma}\,b + (1 - \bar{\sigma})\,d \;=\; \pi^* \quad \text{(C.62)}$$

holds. Note that due to (C.62) and $\pi^* > d$ the denominator in $\frac{\pi^* - (\bar{\sigma}b + (1 - \bar{\sigma})d)}{2\pi^* - (\bar{\sigma}b + (1 - \bar{\sigma})d) - d}$ is strictly positive.

ii. If $\sigma_e > \bar{\sigma}$ and $\sigma_e \neq \sigma^*$, then $\sigma_i = 1$. We have

$$
\begin{aligned}
\Pi_{T'}((1-\epsilon)\,\delta_{T'} + \epsilon\,\delta_{T_e} \mid \bar{b}) &- \Pi_{T_e}((1-\epsilon)\,\delta_{T'} + \epsilon\,\delta_{T_e} \mid \bar{b}) \\
&= (1-\epsilon)\,(\pi^* - (\sigma_e\,a + (1-\sigma_e)\,c)) \\
&\quad + \epsilon\,(\sigma_e\,a + (1-\sigma_e)\,b - \pi(\sigma_3, \sigma_3)) \\
&\geq (1-\epsilon)\,(\pi^* - (\sigma_e\,a + (1-\sigma_e)\,c)) \\
&\quad + \epsilon\,(\sigma_e\,a + (1-\sigma_e)\,c - \pi^*) \\
&= (1-2\epsilon)\,(\pi^* - (\sigma_e\,a + (1-\sigma_e)\,c)),
\end{aligned}
\tag{C.63}
$$

which is always positive for $\epsilon \in (0, \frac{1}{2})$ since

$$
\sigma_e\,a + (1-\sigma_e)\,c \;\leq\; \bar{\sigma}\,a + (1-\bar{\sigma})\,c \;=\; \pi^*
\tag{C.64}
$$

holds.

iii. If $\sigma_e = \sigma^*$, then $\sigma_i \in [\sigma^*, 1]$ must hold. One verifies from $\bar{\sigma} < \sigma^*$ and (C.52) that

$$
\sigma^* a + (1-\sigma^*)\,c < \pi^* < \sigma^* b + (1-\sigma^*)\,d
\tag{C.65}
$$

and

$$
\sigma^* a + (1-\sigma^*)\,b > \pi^* > \sigma^* c + (1-\sigma^*)\,d
\tag{C.66}
$$

hold true. Therefore, for any $\sigma_i \in [\sigma^*, 1]$ we have

$$
\begin{aligned}
\pi(\sigma_e, \sigma_i) &= \sigma_i\,[\sigma^* a + (1-\sigma^*)\,c] \\
&\quad + (1-\sigma_i)\,[\sigma^* b + (1-\sigma^*)\,d] \\
&\leq \pi^*
\end{aligned}
\tag{C.67}
$$

and

$$
\begin{aligned}
\pi(\sigma_i, \sigma_e) &= \sigma_i\,[\sigma^* a + (1-\sigma^*)\,b] \\
&\quad + (1-\sigma_i)\,[\sigma^* c + (1-\sigma^*)\,d] \\
&\geq \pi^*,
\end{aligned}
\tag{C.68}
$$

with equalities if and only if $\sigma_i = \sigma^*$. It follows that

$$
\begin{aligned}
\Pi_{T'}((1-\epsilon)\,\delta_{T'} + \epsilon\,\delta_{T_e} \mid \bar{b}) \\
\geq \pi^* \\
\geq \Pi_{T_e}((1-\epsilon)\,\delta_{T'} + \epsilon\,\delta_{T_e} \mid \bar{b})
\end{aligned}
\tag{C.69}
$$

holds independently of the size of ϵ. The average fitness generated by the entrant never exceeds that of the incumbent type.

iv. If $\sigma_e = \bar{\sigma}$, then $\sigma_i \in [0,1]$ and we have

$$
\begin{aligned}
\pi(\sigma_e, \sigma_i) &= \sigma_i \left[\bar{\sigma} \ a + (1 - \bar{\sigma}) \ c\right] \\
&\quad + (1 - \sigma_i) \left[\bar{\sigma} \ b + (1 - \bar{\sigma}) \ d\right] \\
&= \sigma_i \ \pi^* + (1 - \sigma_i) \left[\bar{\sigma} \ b + (1 - \bar{\sigma}) \ d\right] \qquad \text{(C.70)} \\
&\leq \sigma_i \ \pi^* + (1 - \sigma_i) \left[\bar{\bar{\sigma}} \ b + (1 - \bar{\bar{\sigma}}) \ d\right] \\
&= \pi^*,
\end{aligned}
$$

with equality if and only if $\sigma_i = 1$, and

$$
\pi(\sigma_i, \sigma_e) = \sigma_i \left[\bar{\sigma} \ a + (1 - \bar{\sigma}) \ b\right] + (1 - \sigma_i) \left[\bar{\sigma} \ c + (1 - \bar{\sigma}) \ d\right]. \quad \text{(C.71)}
$$

There exists $\sigma' \in (0,1)$ such that we have $\pi(\sigma_i, \sigma_e) > \pi(\sigma_e, \sigma_i)$ for $\sigma_i \in (\sigma', \ 1]$ and $\pi(\sigma_i, \sigma_e) \leq \pi(\sigma_e, \sigma_i)$ for $\sigma_i \in [0, \ \sigma']$. In the former case it follows that that $\Pi_{T'}(\cdot) \geq \Pi_{T_e}(\cdot)$ holds whenever $\epsilon \in (0, \frac{1}{2})$. In the latter case we have

$$
\begin{aligned}
\Pi_{T'}&((1 - \epsilon) \ \delta_{T'} + \epsilon \ \delta_{T_e} \mid \bar{b}) - \Pi_{T_e}((1 - \epsilon) \ \delta_{T'} + \epsilon \ \delta_{T_e} \mid \bar{b}) \\
&\geq (1 - \epsilon) \ (\pi^* - (\sigma_i \ \pi^* + (1 - \sigma_i) \left[\bar{\sigma} \ b + (1 - \bar{\sigma}) \ d\right])) \\
&\quad + \epsilon \ (\sigma_i \left[\bar{\sigma} \ a + (1 - \bar{\sigma}) \ b\right] \\
&\quad\quad + (1 - \sigma_i) \left[\bar{\sigma} \ c + (1 - \bar{\sigma}) \ d\right] - \pi^*), \\
&\geq (1 - \epsilon) \ (\pi^* - (\sigma' \ \pi^* + (1 - \sigma') \left[\bar{\sigma} \ b + (1 - \bar{\sigma}) \ d\right])) \\
&\quad + \epsilon \ (\left[\bar{\sigma} \ c + (1 - \bar{\sigma}) \ d\right] - \pi^*),
\end{aligned}
$$

(C.72)

where the latter expression is strictly positive for any $\epsilon \in (0, \epsilon'')$ with

$$
\epsilon'' \equiv \frac{\pi^* - (\sigma' \ \pi^* + (1 - \sigma') \left[\bar{\sigma} \ b + (1 - \bar{\sigma}) \ d\right])}{2\pi^* - (\sigma' \ \pi^* + (1 - \sigma') \left[\bar{\sigma} \ b + (1 - \bar{\sigma}) \ d\right]) - \left[\bar{\sigma} \ b + (1 - \bar{\sigma}) \ d\right]}. \quad \text{(C.73)}
$$

Therefore, we define $\bar{\epsilon}$ as the minimum of the invasion barriers derived in i. to iv. It follows that for any $T_e \notin C(\delta_{T'})$, $\epsilon \in (0, \bar{\epsilon})$ and $\bar{b} \in B((1 - \epsilon) \ \delta_{T'} + \epsilon \ \delta_{T_e})$ the average fitness generated by an entrant T_e can never exceed that of the incumbent type T' since the former enters in sufficiently small proportion.

2nd case: $b > c$ and $\pi^* > c$. Consider a monomorphic population in which the only type T_{1,σ^*} generates a best-response correspondence $\beta_{T_{1,\sigma^*}}$ as follows:

$$\beta_{T_{1,\sigma^*}}(\sigma) = \begin{cases} [\sigma^*,\ 1] & \text{if } \sigma = \sigma^* \\ \{1\} & \text{otherwise} \end{cases}. \tag{C.74}$$

The pure strategy A is a weakly dominant strategy for agents of this type. Such an agent randomizes only if its opponent chooses the strategy $\sigma^* \in \Delta$. We have already seen in the 3rd case of the proof of Lemma 5.14 that type T_{1,σ^*} is well-defined since a preference relation in $\mathcal{T}_{\mathcal{R}}$ inducing the best-response correspondence defined in (C.74) in fact exists.

Now, consider the equilibrium configuration b in which $b_{T_{1,\sigma^*}}(T_{1,\sigma^*}) = \sigma^*$, i.e. where all agents play the strategy σ^* in all their interactions. We claim that this monomorphic population together with b is stable w.r.t. the fitness function π. Let an entrant type, say T_e, into the population be such that in the post-entry equilibrium configuration $\bar{b}$ the Nash equilibrium which is played between an entrant-type agent and an incumbent-type agent is $(\sigma_e, \sigma_i) \equiv (\bar{b}_{T_e}(T_{1,\sigma^*}), \bar{b}_{T_{1,\sigma^*}}(T_e))$ and the Nash equilibrium between two entrant-type agents is $(\sigma_3, \sigma_3) \equiv (\bar{b}_{T_e}(T_e), \bar{b}_{T_e}(T_e))$. The average fitness generated by the incumbent and the entrant are, respectively, given by

$$\Pi_{T_{1,\sigma^*}}((1-\epsilon)\,\delta_{T_{1,\sigma^*}} + \epsilon\,\delta_{T_e} \mid \bar{b}) = (1-\epsilon)\,\pi^* + \epsilon\,\pi(\sigma_i, \sigma_e) \tag{C.75}$$

and

$$\begin{aligned} \Pi_{T_e}((1-\epsilon)\,\delta_{T_{1,\sigma^*}} + \epsilon\,\delta_{T_e} \mid \bar{b}) \\ = (1-\epsilon)\,\pi(\sigma_e, \sigma_i) + \epsilon\,\pi(\sigma_3, \sigma_3). \end{aligned} \tag{C.76}$$

i. If $\sigma_e \neq \sigma^*$, then $\sigma_i = 1$. We have

$$\begin{aligned} \Pi_{T_{1,\sigma^*}}((1-\epsilon)\,&\delta_{T_{1,\sigma^*}} + \epsilon\,\delta_{T_e} \mid \bar{b}) \\ &- \Pi_{T_e}((1-\epsilon)\,\delta_{T_{1,\sigma^*}} + \epsilon\,\delta_{T_e} \mid \bar{b}) \\ =\ &(1-\epsilon)\,(\pi^* - (\sigma_e\,a + (1-\sigma_e)\,c)) \\ &+ \epsilon\,(\sigma_e\,a + (1-\sigma_e)\,b - \pi(\sigma_3, \sigma_3)) \\ \geq\ &(1-\epsilon)\,(\pi^* - (\sigma_e\,a + (1-\sigma_e)\,c)) \\ &+ \epsilon\,(\sigma_e\,a + (1-\sigma_e)\,c - \pi^*) \\ =\ &(1-2\epsilon)\,(\pi^* - (\sigma_e\,a + (1-\sigma_e)\,c)), \end{aligned} \tag{C.77}$$

which is always positive for $\epsilon \in (0, \frac{1}{2})$ because we have $\pi^* > a$ and $\pi^* > c$.

ii. If $\sigma_e = \sigma^*$, then for any $\sigma_i \in [\sigma^*, 1]$ we have

$$\pi(\sigma_e, \sigma_i) = \sigma_i \left[\sigma^* a + (1 - \sigma^*) c\right]$$
$$+ (1 - \sigma_i) \left[\sigma^* b + (1 - \sigma^*) d\right] \qquad (C.78)$$
$$\leq \pi^*$$

and

$$\pi(\sigma_i, \sigma_e) = \sigma_i \left[\sigma^* a + (1 - \sigma^*) b\right]$$
$$+ (1 - \sigma_i) \left[\sigma^* c + (1 - \sigma^*) d\right] \qquad (C.79)$$
$$\geq \pi^*,$$

with equalities if and only if $\sigma_i = \sigma^*$. It follows that

$$\Pi_{T_{1,\sigma^*}} ((1 - \epsilon) \, \delta_{T_{1,\sigma^*}} + \epsilon \, \delta_{T_e} \mid \bar{b})$$
$$\geq \pi^* \geq \Pi_{T_e} ((1 - \epsilon) \, \delta_{T_{1,\sigma^*}} + \epsilon \, \delta_{T_e} \mid \bar{b}) \qquad (C.80)$$

holds independently of the size of ϵ. The average fitness generated by the entrant never exceeds that of the incumbent type.

Therefore, for any $T_e \notin C(\delta_{T_{1,\sigma^*}})$, $\epsilon \in (0, \frac{1}{2})$ and $\bar{b} \in B((1 - \epsilon) \, \delta_{T_{1,\sigma^*}} + \epsilon \, \delta_{T_e})$ the average fitness generated by an entrant T_e can never exceed that of the incumbent type T_{1,σ^*} since the former enters in sufficiently small proportion.

3rd case: $c > b \geq \pi^*$. Consider a monomorphic population in which the only type T'' generates a best-response correspondence $\beta_{T''}$ as follows:

$$\beta_{T''}(\sigma) = \begin{cases} \{1\} & \text{if } \sigma > \bar{\sigma} + \eta \\ [0,1] & \text{if } \sigma = \bar{\sigma} + \eta \\ [0, \sigma^*] & \text{if } \sigma = \sigma^* \\ \{0\} & \text{if } \sigma < \bar{\sigma} + \eta \text{ and } \sigma \neq \sigma^* \end{cases}, \qquad (C.81)$$

where $\eta \equiv \frac{\bar{\bar{\sigma}} - \bar{\sigma}}{2} > 0$. As $c > b$ we know from the 1st case that $\sigma^* < \bar{\sigma} < \bar{\sigma} + \eta$ must hold. The type T'' is well-defined since a preference relation in $\mathcal{T}_R$ inducing the best-response correspondence defined in (C.81) in fact exists. Take, for instance, a preference relation $\succsim_{T''}$ which is represented by the utility function $u_{T''} : \Delta \times \Delta \to \mathbb{R}$ defined by

$$u_{T''}(\sigma_T, \sigma_{-T}) = (\sigma_{-T} - \bar{\sigma} - \eta)\,(\sigma_T\,|\sigma_{-T} - \sigma^*| + \max\{\sigma_T - \sigma^*, 0\}). \quad \text{(C.82)}$$

This preference relation is continuous since $u_{T'}$ is continuous. It also satisfies betweenness in the first component because for any $\bar{\sigma}_{-T} \in \Delta$ we have that $u_{T''}(\,\cdot\,, \bar{\sigma}_{-T})$ is a monotone (i.e. increasing or decreasing) function.

Now, consider the equilibrium configuration b in which $b_{T''}(T'') = \sigma^*$, i.e. where all agents play the strategy σ^* in all their interactions. We claim that this monomorphic population together with b is stable w.r.t. the fitness function π. Let an entrant type, say T_e, into the population be such that in the post-entry equilibrium configuration $\bar{b}$ the Nash equilibrium which is played between an entrant-type agent and an incumbent-type agent is $(\sigma_e, \sigma_i) \equiv (\bar{b}_{T_e}(T''), \bar{b}_{T''}(T_e))$ and the Nash equilibrium between two entrant-type agents is $(\sigma_3, \sigma_3) \equiv (\bar{b}_{T_e}(T_e), \bar{b}_{T_e}(T_e))$. The average fitness generated by the incumbent and the entrant are, respectively, given by

$$\Pi_{T''}((1-\epsilon)\,\delta_{T''} + \epsilon\,\delta_{T_e} \mid \bar{b}) = (1-\epsilon)\,\pi^* + \epsilon\,\pi(\sigma_i, \sigma_e) \quad \text{(C.83)}$$

and

$$\Pi_{T_e}((1-\epsilon)\,\delta_{T''} + \epsilon\,\delta_{T_e} \mid \bar{b}) = (1-\epsilon)\,\pi(\sigma_e, \sigma_i) + \epsilon\,\pi(\sigma_3, \sigma_3). \quad \text{(C.84)}$$

i. If $\sigma_e < \bar{\sigma} + \eta$ and $\sigma_e \neq \sigma^*$, then $\sigma_i = 0$. We have

$$\begin{aligned}
\Pi_{T''}&((1-\epsilon)\,\delta_{T''} + \epsilon\,\delta_{T_e} \mid \bar{b}) - \Pi_{T_e}((1-\epsilon)\,\delta_{T''} + \epsilon\,\delta_{T_e} \mid \bar{b}) \\
&= (1-\epsilon)\,(\pi^* - (\sigma_e\,b + (1-\sigma_e)\,d)) \\
&\quad + \epsilon\,(\sigma_e\,c + (1-\sigma_e)\,d - \pi(\sigma_3, \sigma_3)) \\
&\geq (1-\epsilon)\,(\pi^* - (\sigma_e\,b + (1-\sigma_e)\,d)) \\
&\quad + \epsilon\,(\sigma_e\,b + (1-\sigma_e)\,d - \pi^*) \\
&= (1-2\epsilon)\,(\pi^* - (\sigma_e\,b + (1-\sigma_e)\,d)),
\end{aligned} \quad \text{(C.85)}$$

which is always positive for $\epsilon \in (0, \frac{1}{2})$ since

$$\begin{aligned}
\sigma_e\,b + (1-\sigma_e)\,d &\leq (\bar{\sigma} + \eta)\,b + (1 - (\bar{\sigma} + \eta))\,d \\
&< \bar{\sigma}\,b + (1 - \bar{\sigma})\,d \\
&= \pi^*
\end{aligned} \quad \text{(C.86)}$$

holds.

ii. If $\sigma_e > \bar{\sigma} + \eta$, then $\sigma_i = 1$. We have

$$\Pi_{T''}((1-\epsilon)\,\delta_{T''} + \epsilon\,\delta_{T_e} \mid \bar{b}) - \Pi_{T_e}((1-\epsilon)\,\delta_{T''} + \epsilon\,\delta_{T_e} \mid \bar{b})$$

$$= (1-\epsilon)\,(\pi^* - (\sigma_e\,a + (1-\sigma_e)\,c))$$

$$+ \epsilon\,(\sigma_e\,a + (1-\sigma_e)\,b - \pi(\sigma_3,\sigma_3)) \qquad (C.87)$$

$$> (1-\epsilon)\,(\pi^* - ((\bar{\sigma}+\eta)\,a + (1-(\bar{\sigma}+\eta))\,c))$$

$$+ \epsilon\,(a - \pi^*),$$

where the latter expression is positive for any

$$\epsilon \in \left(0,\; \frac{\pi^* - ((\bar{\sigma}+\eta)a + (1-(\bar{\sigma}+\eta))c)}{2\pi^* - ((\bar{\sigma}+\eta)a + (1-(\bar{\sigma}+\eta))c) - a}\right) \qquad (C.88)$$

because

$$(\bar{\sigma}+\eta)\,a + (1-(\bar{\sigma}+\eta))\,c \;<\; \bar{\sigma}\,a + (1-\bar{\sigma})\,c \;=\; \pi^* \qquad (C.89)$$

holds. Note that due to (C.89) and $\pi^* > a$ (since A is not efficient) the denominator in $\frac{\pi^* - ((\bar{\sigma}+\eta)a + (1-(\bar{\sigma}+\eta))c)}{2\pi^* - ((\bar{\sigma}+\eta)a + (1-(\bar{\sigma}+\eta))c) - a}$ is strictly positive.

iii. If $\sigma_e = \sigma^*$, then $\sigma_i \in [0,\sigma^*]$ must hold. One verifies from $\bar{\bar{\sigma}} > \bar{\sigma} > \sigma^*$ and (C.52) that

$$\sigma^* a + (1-\sigma^*)\,c > \pi^* > \sigma^* b + (1-\sigma^*)\,d \qquad (C.90)$$

and

$$\sigma^* a + (1-\sigma^*)\,b < \pi^* < \sigma^* c + (1-\sigma^*)\,d \qquad (C.91)$$

hold true. Therefore, for any $\sigma_i \in [0,\sigma^*]$ we have

$$\pi(\sigma_e,\sigma_i) = \sigma_i\,[\sigma^* a + (1-\sigma^*)\,c]$$

$$+ (1-\sigma_i)\,[\sigma^* b + (1-\sigma^*)\,d] \qquad (C.92)$$

$$\leq \pi^*$$

and

$$\pi(\sigma_i,\sigma_e) = \sigma_i\,[\sigma^* a + (1-\sigma^*)\,b]$$

$$+ (1-\sigma_i)\,[\sigma^* c + (1-\sigma^*)\,d] \qquad (C.93)$$

$$\geq \pi^*,$$

with equalities if and only if $\sigma_i = \sigma^*$. It follows that

$$\Pi_{T''}((1 - \epsilon)\, \delta_{T''} + \epsilon\, \delta_{T_e} \mid \bar{b})$$

$$\geq \pi^* \geq \Pi_{T_e}((1 - \epsilon)\, \delta_{T''} + \epsilon\, \delta_{T_e} \mid \bar{b}) \tag{C.94}$$

holds independently of the size of ϵ. The average fitness generated by the entrant never exceeds that of the incumbent type.

iv. If $\sigma_e = \bar{\sigma} + \eta$, then $\sigma_i \in [0, 1]$ and we have

$$\pi(\sigma_e, \sigma_i) = \sigma_i\, [(\bar{\sigma} + \eta)\, a + (1 - (\bar{\sigma} + \eta))\, c]$$

$$+ (1 - \sigma_i)\, [(\bar{\sigma} + \eta)\, b + (1 - (\bar{\sigma} + \eta))\, d]$$

$$< \sigma_i\, [\bar{\sigma}\, a + (1 - \bar{\sigma})\, c] \tag{C.95}$$

$$+ (1 - \sigma_i)\, [\bar{\bar{\sigma}}\, b + (1 - \bar{\bar{\sigma}})\, d]$$

$$= \pi^*$$

and

$$\pi(\sigma_i, \sigma_e) = \sigma_i\, [(\bar{\sigma} + \eta)\, a + (1 - (\bar{\sigma} + \eta))\, b]$$

$$+ (1 - \sigma_i)\, [(\bar{\sigma} + \eta)\, c + (1 - (\bar{\sigma} + \eta))\, d]. \tag{C.96}$$

There exists $\sigma'' \in (0, 1)$ such that we have $\pi(\sigma_i, \sigma_e) > \pi(\sigma_e, \sigma_i)$ for $\sigma_i \in [0, \sigma'')$ and $\pi(\sigma_i, \sigma_e) \leq \pi(\sigma_e, \sigma_i)$ for $\sigma_i \in [\sigma', 1]$. In the former case it follows that that $\Pi_{T''}(\cdot) \geq \Pi_{T_e}(\cdot)$ holds whenever $\epsilon \in (0, \frac{1}{2})$. In the latter case we have

$$\Pi_{T''}((1 - \epsilon)\, \delta_{T''} + \epsilon\, \delta_{T_e} \mid \bar{b}) - \Pi_{T_e}((1 - \epsilon)\, \delta_{T''} + \epsilon\, \delta_{T_e} \mid \bar{b})$$

$$\geq (1 - \epsilon)\, (\pi^* - \pi(\bar{\sigma} + \eta, \sigma_i)) + \epsilon\, (\pi(\sigma_i, \bar{\sigma} + \eta) - \pi^*)$$

$$\geq (1 - \epsilon)\, (\pi^* - \max_{\sigma_i \in [\sigma', 1]} \pi(\bar{\sigma} + \eta, \sigma_i)) \tag{C.97}$$

$$+ \epsilon\, (\min_{\sigma_i \in [\sigma', 1]} \pi(\sigma_i, \bar{\sigma} + \eta) - \pi^*),$$

where the latter expression is strictly positive for any $\epsilon \in (0, \epsilon'')$ with ϵ'' being defined by

$$\epsilon'' \equiv \frac{\pi^* - \max_{\sigma_i \in [\sigma', 1]} \pi(\bar{\sigma} + \eta, \sigma_i)}{2\pi^* - \max_{\sigma_i \in [\sigma', 1]} \pi(\bar{\sigma} + \eta, \sigma_i) - \min_{\sigma_i \in [\sigma', 1]} \pi(\sigma_i, \bar{\sigma} + \eta)}. \tag{C.98}$$

Note that ϵ'' is strictly positive.

Therefore, we define $\bar{\epsilon}'$ as the minimum of the invasion barriers derived in *i.* to *iv.* It follows that for any $T_e \notin C(\delta_{T''})$, $\epsilon \in (0, \bar{\epsilon}')$

and $\bar{b} \in B((1 - \epsilon)\ \delta_{T''} + \epsilon\ \delta_{T_e})$ the average fitness generated by an entrant T_e can never exceed that of the incumbent type T'' since the former enters in sufficiently small proportion.

4th case: $c > b$ and $\pi^* > b$. Consider a monomorphic population in which the only type T_{0,σ^*} generates a best-response correspondence $\beta_{T_{0,\sigma^*}}$ as follows:

$$\beta_{T_{0,\sigma^*}}(\sigma) = \begin{cases} [0,\ \sigma^*] & \text{if } \sigma = \sigma^* \\ \{0\} & \text{otherwise} \end{cases}. \tag{C.99}$$

The pure strategy B is a weakly dominant strategy for agents of this type. Such an agent randomizes only if its opponent chooses the strategy $\sigma^* \in \Delta$. We have already seen in the 2nd case of the proof of Lemma 5.14 that type T_{0,σ^*} is well-defined since a preference relation in $\mathcal{T_R}$ inducing the best-response correspondence defined in (C.99) in fact exists.

Now, consider the equilibrium configuration b in which $b_{T_{0,\sigma^*}}(T_{0,\sigma^*}) = \sigma^*$, i.e. where all agents play the strategy σ^* in all their interactions. We claim that this monomorphic population together with b is stable w.r.t. the fitness function π. Let an entrant type, say T_e, into the population be such that in the post-entry equilibrium configuration $\bar{b}$ the Nash equilibrium which is played between an entrant-type agent and an incumbent-type agent is $(\sigma_e, \sigma_i) \equiv (\bar{b}_{T_e}(T_{0,\sigma^*}), \bar{b}_{T_{0,\sigma^*}}(T_e))$ and the Nash equilibrium between two entrant-type agent is $(\sigma_3, \sigma_3) \equiv (\bar{b}_{T_e}(T_e), \bar{b}_{T_e}(T_e))$. The average fitness generated by the incumbent and the entrant are, respectively, given by

$$\Pi_{T_{0,\sigma^*}}((1-\epsilon)\ \delta_{T_{0,\sigma^*}} + \epsilon\ \delta_{T_e} \mid \bar{b}) = (1-\epsilon)\ \pi^* + \epsilon\ \pi(\sigma_i, \sigma_e) \tag{C.100}$$

and

$$\Pi_{T_e}((1-\epsilon)\ \delta_{T_{0,\sigma^*}} + \epsilon\ \delta_{T_e} \mid \bar{b})$$
$$= (1-\epsilon)\ \pi(\sigma_e, \sigma_i) + \epsilon\ \pi(\sigma_3, \sigma_3). \tag{C.101}$$

i. If $\sigma_e \neq \sigma^*$, then $\sigma_i = 0$. We have

$$\Pi_{T_{0,\sigma^*}}((1-\epsilon)\,\delta_{T_{0,\sigma^*}} + \epsilon\,\delta_{T_e} \mid \bar{b})$$

$$-\Pi_{T_e}((1-\epsilon)\,\delta_{T_{0,\sigma^*}} + \epsilon\,\delta_{T_e} \mid \bar{b})$$

$$= (1-\epsilon)\,(\pi^* - (\sigma_e\,b + (1-\sigma_e)\,d))$$

$$+ \epsilon\,(\sigma_e\,c + (1-\sigma_e)\,d - \pi(\sigma_3, \sigma_3)) \qquad \text{(C.102)}$$

$$\geq (1-\epsilon)\,(\pi^* - (\sigma_e\,b + (1-\sigma_e)\,d))$$

$$+ \epsilon\,(\sigma_e\,b + (1-\sigma_e)\,d - \pi^*)$$

$$= (1-2\epsilon)\,(\pi^* - (\sigma_e\,b + (1-\sigma_e)\,d)),$$

which is always positive for $\epsilon \in (0, \frac{1}{2})$ because we have $\pi^* > a \geq d$ and $\pi^* > b$.

ii. If $\sigma_e = \sigma^*$, then for any $\sigma_i \in [0, \sigma^*]$ we have

$$\pi(\sigma_e, \sigma_i) = \sigma_i\,[\sigma^*a + (1-\sigma^*)\,c]$$

$$+ (1-\sigma_i)\,[\sigma^*b + (1-\sigma^*)\,d] \qquad \text{(C.103)}$$

$$\leq \pi^*$$

and

$$\pi(\sigma_i, \sigma_e) = \sigma_i\,[\sigma^*a + (1-\sigma^*)\,b]$$

$$+ (1-\sigma_i)\,[\sigma^*c + (1-\sigma^*)\,d] \qquad \text{(C.104)}$$

$$\geq \pi^*,$$

with equalities if and only if $\sigma_i = \sigma^*$. It follows that

$$\Pi_{T_{0,\sigma^*}}((1-\epsilon)\,\delta_{T_{0,\sigma^*}} + \epsilon\,\delta_{T_e} \mid \bar{b})$$

$$\geq \pi^* \geq \Pi_{T_e}((1-\epsilon)\,\delta_{T_{0,\sigma^*}} + \epsilon\,\delta_{T_e} \mid \bar{b}) \qquad \text{(C.105)}$$

holds independently of the size of ϵ. The average fitness generated by the entrant never exceeds that of the incumbent type.

Therefore, for any $T_e \notin C(\delta_{T_{0,\sigma^*}})$, $\epsilon \in (0, \frac{1}{2})$ and $\bar{b} \in B((1-\epsilon)\,\delta_{T_{0,\sigma^*}} + \epsilon\,\delta_{T_e})$ the average fitness generated by an entrant T_e can never exceed that of the incumbent type T_{0,σ^*} since the former enters in sufficiently small proportion.

5th case: $b = c$. This is the only case in which in Dekel et al.'s model with expected utility maximizing types ([14]) efficiency of a mixed strategy w.r.t. π implies stability of that strategy. The related stable population used in their proof ([14], Proposition 3b) can be applied here as well. Consider a monomorphic population in which the only type T_{EU,σ^*} generates a best-response correspondence $\beta_{T_{EU,\sigma^*}}$ as follows:

$$\beta_{T_{EU,\sigma^*}}(\sigma) = \begin{cases} \{1\} & \text{if } \sigma > \sigma^* \\ [0,1] & \text{if } \sigma = \sigma^* \\ \{0\} & \text{if } \sigma < \sigma^* \end{cases}. \tag{C.106}$$

The type T_{EU,σ^*} is well-defined since a preference relation in $\mathcal{T}_{\mathcal{R}}$ inducing the best-response correspondence defined in (C.106) in fact exists. Take, for instance, a preference relation $\succsim_{T_{EU,\sigma^*}}$ which is represented by the utility function $u_{T_{EU,\sigma^*}} : \Delta \times \Delta \to \mathbb{R}$ defined by

$$u_{T_{EU,\sigma^*}}(\sigma_T, \sigma_{-T}) = \sigma_T \left(\sigma_{-T} - \sigma^* \right). \tag{C.107}$$

This preference relation is continuous since $u_{T_{EU,\sigma^*}}$ is continuous. It also satisfies betweenness in the first component because for any $\bar{\sigma}_{-T} \in \Delta$ we have that $u_{T_{EU,\sigma^*}}(\,\cdot\,, \bar{\sigma}_{-T})$ is a monotone function. Note that $u_{T_{EU,\sigma^*}}$ as defined in (C.107) has an expected utility form with a von Neumann-Morgenstern utility function $u_{VNM} : \{A, B\} \times \{A, B\} \to \mathbb{R}$ such that

$$u_{VNM}(A, A) = 1 - \sigma^*,$$

$$u_{VNM}(A, B) = -\sigma^*, \tag{C.108}$$

$$u_{VNM}(B, A) = u_{VNM}(B, B) = 0.$$

Hence, the preference relation T_{EU,σ^*} is in the type space defined by Dekel et. al in [14].

Now, consider the equilibrium configuration b in which $b_{T_{EU,\sigma^*}}(T_{EU,\sigma^*}) = \sigma^*$, i.e. where all agents play the strategy σ^* in all their interactions. We claim that this monomorphic population together with b is stable w.r.t. the fitness function π. Let an entrant type, say T_e, into the population be such that in the post-entry equilibrium configuration $\bar{b}$ the Nash equilibrium which is played between an entrant-type agent and an incumbent-type agent is $(\sigma_e, \sigma_i) \equiv (\bar{b}_{T_e}(T_{EU,\sigma^*}), \bar{b}_{T_{EU,\sigma^*}}(T_e))$ and the Nash equilibrium between two entrant-type agents is $(\sigma_3, \sigma_3) \equiv (\bar{b}_{T_e}(T_e), \bar{b}_{T_e}(T_e))$. The average fitness generated by the incumbent and the entrant are, respectively, given by

$$\Pi_{T_{EU,\sigma^*}}((1-\epsilon)\,\delta_{T_{EU,\sigma^*}} + \epsilon\,\delta_{T_e} \mid \bar{b})$$
$$= (1-\epsilon)\,\pi^* + \epsilon\,\pi(\sigma_i,\sigma_e) \qquad (C.109)$$

and

$$\Pi_{T_e}((1-\epsilon)\,\delta_{T_{EU,\sigma^*}} + \epsilon\,\delta_{T_e} \mid \bar{b})$$
$$= (1-\epsilon)\,\pi(\sigma_e,\sigma_i) + \epsilon\,\pi(\sigma_3,\sigma_3). \qquad (C.110)$$

As $b = c$ we have that in any match both players' fitness is always identical. In particular, $\pi(\sigma_e,\sigma_i) = \pi(\sigma_i,\sigma_e)$ must necessarily hold.

i. If $\sigma_e < \sigma^*$, then $\sigma_i = 0$. Hence, $b = c > a \geq d$ implies

$$\pi(\sigma_i,\sigma_e) = \pi(\sigma_e,\sigma_i)$$

$$= \sigma_e\,b + (1-\sigma_e)\,d$$

$$< \sigma^*\,b + (1-\sigma^*)\,d$$

$$= d + \sigma^*(b-d) \qquad (C.111)$$

$$= d + \frac{2b-2d}{2\,(2b-a-d)}\,(b-d)$$

$$= d + \frac{(2b-2d)^2}{4\,(2b-a-d)}$$

$$= \pi^*.$$

It follows that

$$\Pi_{T_{EU,\sigma^*}}((1-\epsilon)\,\delta_{T_{EU,\sigma^*}} + \epsilon\,\delta_{T_e} \mid \bar{b})$$
$$= (1-\epsilon)\,\pi^* + \epsilon\,\pi(\sigma_e,\sigma_i) \qquad (C.112)$$

and

$$\Pi_{T_e}((1-\epsilon)\,\delta_{T_{EU,\sigma^*}} + \epsilon\,\delta_{T_e} \mid \bar{b})$$
$$\leq (1-\epsilon)\,\pi(\sigma_e,\sigma_i) + \epsilon\,\pi^*. \qquad (C.113)$$

For any $\epsilon \in (0,\frac{1}{2})$ we have $\Pi_{T_{EU,\sigma^*}}(.) \geq \Pi_{T_e}(.)$.

ii. If $\sigma_e > \sigma^*$, then $\sigma_i = 1$. Hence, we have

$$\pi(\sigma_i, \sigma_e) = \pi(\sigma_e, \sigma_i)$$
$$= \sigma_e \, a + (1 - \sigma_e) \, c$$
$$= \sigma_e \, a + (1 - \sigma_e) \, b \tag{C.114}$$
$$< \sigma^* \, a + (1 - \sigma^*) \, b$$
$$= \pi^*.$$

The latter equality holds because we have

$$\pi^* = \sigma^* \left[\sigma^* a + (1 - \sigma^*) \, c\right] + (1 - \sigma^*) \left[\sigma^* b + (1 - \sigma^*) \, d\right]$$
$$= \sigma^* \left[\sigma^* a + (1 - \sigma^*) \, b\right] + (1 - \sigma^*) \left[\sigma^* b + (1 - \sigma^*) \, d\right] \tag{C.115}$$
$$= \sigma^* \left[\sigma^* a + (1 - \sigma^*) \, b\right] + (1 - \sigma^*) \, \pi^*.$$

It follows that

$$\Pi_{T_{EU,\sigma^*}}((1 - \epsilon) \, \delta_{T_{EU,\sigma^*}} + \epsilon \, \delta_{T_e} \mid \bar{b})$$
$$= (1 - \epsilon) \, \pi^* + \epsilon \, \pi(\sigma_e, \sigma_i) \tag{C.116}$$

and

$$\Pi_{T_e}((1 - \epsilon) \, \delta_{T_{EU,\sigma^*}} + \epsilon \, \delta_{T_e} \mid \bar{b})$$
$$\leq (1 - \epsilon) \, \pi(\sigma_e, \sigma_i) + \epsilon \, \pi^*. \tag{C.117}$$

For any $\epsilon \in (0, \frac{1}{2})$ we have $\Pi_{T_{EU,\sigma^*}}(.) \geq \Pi_{T_e}(.)$.

iii. If $\sigma_e = \sigma^*$, then $\sigma_i \in [0, 1]$ and we have

$$\pi(\sigma_i, \sigma_e) = \pi(\sigma_e, \sigma_i) = \pi(\sigma^*, \sigma_i)$$
$$= \sigma_i \left[\sigma^* a + (1 - \sigma^*) \, c\right] + (1 - \sigma_i) \left[\sigma^* b + (1 - \sigma^*) \, d\right]$$
$$= \sigma_i \, \pi^* + (1 - \sigma_i) \, \pi^*$$
$$= \pi^*.$$

It follows that

$$\Pi_{T_{EU,\sigma^*}}((1 - \epsilon) \, \delta_{T_{EU,\sigma^*}} + \epsilon \, \delta_{T_e} \mid \bar{b})$$
$$= \pi^*$$
$$\geq (1 - \epsilon) \, \pi^* + \epsilon \, \pi(\sigma_3, \sigma_3) \tag{C.118}$$
$$= \Pi_{T_e}((1 - \epsilon) \, \delta_{T_{EU,\sigma^*}} + \epsilon \, \delta_{T_e} \mid \bar{b})$$

holds independently of the size of ϵ. The average fitness generated by the entrant never exceeds that of the incumbent type.

Therefore, for any $T_e \notin C(\delta_{T_{EU,\sigma^*}})$, $\epsilon \in (0, \frac{1}{2})$ and $\bar{b} \in B((1-\epsilon)$ $\delta_{T_{EU,\sigma^*}} + \epsilon \, \delta_{T_e})$ the average fitness generated by an entrant T_e can never exceed that of the incumbent type T_{EU,σ^*} since the former enters in sufficiently small proportion.   □

References

1. Akin E (1980) Domination or equilibrium. Mathematical Biosciences 50:239–250
2. Allais M (1953) Le comportement de l'homme rationnel devant le risque: critique des postulats et axiomes de l'ecole americaine. Econometrica 21:503–546
3. Anscombe FJ, Aumann RJ (1963) A definition of subjective probability. Annals of Mathematical Statistics 34:199–205
4. Bester H, Güth W (1998) Is altruism evolutionarily stable? Journal of Economic Behavior and Organization 4(2):193–209
5. Camerer C (2003) Behavioral game theory: experiments in strategic interaction. Princeton University Press, Princeton
6. Camerer CF, Ho T-H (1994) Violations of the betweenness axiom and nonlinearity in probability. Journal of Risk and Uncertainty 8:167–196
7. Charness G, Rabin M (2002) Understanding social preferences with simple tests. Quarterly Journal of Economics 117(3):817–869
8. Chateauneuf A, Cohen M (1994) Risk seeking with diminishing marginal utility in a non-expected utility model. Journal of Risk and Uncertainty 9:77–91
9. Chew SH, Karni E, Safra Z (1987) Risk aversion in the theory of expected utility with rank dependent probabilities. Journal of Economic Theory 42:370–381
10. Cooper, WS (1987) Decision theory as a branch of evolutionary theory: a biological derivation of the Savage axioms. Psychological Review 94:395–411
11. Darwin C (1859) On the origin of species by means of natural selection, or the preservation of favoured races in the struggle for life. First edition. John Murray, London
12. Debreu G (1971) Theory of value: an axiomatic analysis of economic equilibrium. Fourth printing. Yale University Press, New Haven London
13. Dekel E (1989) Asset demands without the independence axiom. Econometrica 57:163–169

14. Dekel E, Ely JC, Yilankaya O (2007) Evolution of preferences. Review of Economic Studies 74:685–704
15. Dekel E, Scotchmer S (1992) On the evolution of optimizing behavior. Journal of Economic Theory 57:392–406
16. Diecidue E, Wakker PP (2001) On the intuition of rank-dependent utility. Journal of Risk and Uncertainty 23(3):281–298
17. Ely JC, Yilankaya O (2001) Nash equilibrium and the evolution of preferences. Journal of Economic Theory 97:255–272
18. Frank RH (1988) Passions within reason - the strategic role of the emotions. Norton, New York
19. Fudenberg D, Tirole J (1991) Game theory. MIT Press, Cambridge London
20. Gintis H (2000) Game theory evolving. Princeton University Press, Princeton
21. Gonzalez R, Wu G (1999) On the shape of the probability weighting function. Cognitive Psychology 38:129–166
22. Güth W (1995) An evolutionary approach to explaining cooperative behavior by reciprocal incentives. International Journal of Game Theory 24:323–344
23. Güth W, Yaari ME (1992) An evolutionary approach to explain reciprocal behavior in a simple strategic game. In: Witt U (ed) Explaining process and change: approaches in evolutionary economics. The University of Michigan Press, Ann Arbor
24. Hargreaves Heap S, Varoufakis Y (2004) Game theory: a critical text. Second edition. Routledge, London
25. Heifetz A, Shannon C, Spiegel Y (2007) The dynamic evolution of preferences. Economic Theory 32:251-286
26. Hofbauer J, Weibull JW (1996) Evolutionary selection against dominated strategies. Journal of Economic Theory 71:558–573
27. Kahneman D, Tversky A (1979) Prospect theory: an analysis of decision under risk. Econometrica 47(2):263–291
28. Kakutani S (1941) A generalization of brouwer's fixed point theorem. Duke Mathematical Journal 8:457–459
29. Karni E, Schmeidler D (1986) Self-preservation as a foundation of rational behavior under risk. Journal of Economic Behavior and Organization 7:71–81
30. Kreps DM (1988) Notes on the theory of choice. Westview Press, Boulder Oxford
31. Levine DK (1998) Modeling altruism and spitefulness in experiments. Review of Economic Dynamics 1:593–622
32. Losert V, Akin E (1983) Dynamics of games and genes: discrete versus continuous time. Journal of Mathematical Biology 17:241–251
33. Luce RD, Raiffa H (1957) Games and decisions: introduction and critical survey. Wiley, New York

34. MacCrimmon KR, Larsson S (1979) Utility theory: axioms vs. 'paradoxes'. In: Allais M, Hagen O (eds) Expected utility hypotheses and the Allais paradox. D. Reidel Publishing Company, Dordrecht Holland

35. Mailath GJ (1998) Do people play Nash equilibrium? Lessons from evolutionary game theory. Journal of Economic Literature 36:1347–1374

36. Maynard Smith J (1982) Evolution and the theory of games. Cambridge University Press, Cambridge

37. Maynard Smith J, Price GR (1973) The logic of animal instinct. Nature 246:15–18

38. Nash JF Jr (1950) Equilibrium points in n-person games. Proceeding of the National Academy of Science USA 36:48–49

39. von Neumann J, Morgenstern O (1944) Theory of games and economic behavior. Princeton University Press, Princeton

40. Ok EA, Vega-Redondo F (2001) On the evolution of individualistic preferences: an incomplete information scenario. Journal of Economic Theory 97:231–254

41. Osborne MJ, Rubinstein A (1994) A course in game theory. MIT Press, Cambridge London

42. Peleg B, Rosenmüller J, Sudhölter P (1999) The canonical extensive form of a game form: part I - symmetries. In: Alkan A, Aliprantis CD, Yannelis NC (eds) Current trends in economics: theory and applications, studies in economic theory, volume 8. Springer Publishers, New York

43. Possajennikov A (2000) On the evolutionary stability of altruistic and spiteful preferences. Journal of Economic Behavior and Organization 42:125–129

44. Possajennikov A (2004) Two-speed evolution of strategies and preferences in symmetric games. Theory and Decision 57:227–263

45. Quiggin J (1982) A theory of anticipated utility. Journal of Economic Behavior and Organization 3:323–343

46. Ritzberger K (1996) On games under expected utility with rank dependent probabilities. Theory and Decision 40:1–27

47. Robson AJ (1990) Efficiency in evolutionary games: Darwin, Nash and the secret handshake. Journal of Theoretical Biology 144:379–396

48. Robson AJ (1996) A biological basis for expected and non-expected utility. Journal of Economic Theory 68:397–424

49. Robson AJ (2001) The biological basis of economic behavior. Journal of Economic Literature 39:11–33

50. Röell A (1987) Risk aversion in Quiggin and Yaari's rank-order model of choice under uncertainty. The Economic Journal 97(suppl):143–159

51. Sandholm WH (2001) Preference evolution, two-speed dynamics, and rapid social change. Review of Economic Dynamics 4:637–679

52. Savage LJ (1954) The Foundations of Statistics. Wiley, New York

53. Schoemaker P (1982) The expected utility model: its variants, purposes, evidence and limitations. Journal of Economic Literature 20(2):529–563

54. Segal U (1990) Two-stage lotteries without the independence axiom. Econometrica 58: 349-377
55. Selten R (1980) A note on evolutionarily stable strategies in asymmetric animal conflicts. Journal of Theoretical Biology 84:93–101
56. Selten R (1991) Evolution, learning, and economic Behavior. Games and Economic Behavior 3:3–24
57. Sethi R, Somanathan E (2001) Preference evolution and reciprocity. Journal of Economic Theory 97:273–297
58. Starmer C, Sugden R (1989) Violations of the independence axiom in common ratio problems: an experimental test of some competing hypotheses. Annals of Operations Research 19:79–102
59. Swinkels JM (1992) Evolutionary stability with equilibrium entrants. Journal of Economic Theory 57:306–332
60. Taylor P, Jonker L (1978) Evolutionary stable strategies and game dynamics. Mathematical Biosciences 40:145–156
61. Tobin J (1958) Liquidity preference as behavior toward risk. Review of Economic Studies 25:65–86
62. Tversky A, Kahneman D (1992) Advances in prospect theory: cumulative representation of uncertainty. Journal of Risk and Uncertainty 5(4):297–323
63. Wakker PP (1994) Separating marginal utility and probabilistic risk aversion. Theory and Decision 36:1–44
64. Wakker PP, Erev I, Weber EU (1994) Comonotonic independence: the critical test between classical and rank-dependent utility theories. Journal of Risk and Uncertainty 9:195–230
65. Weibull JW (1995) Evolutionary game theory. MIT Press, Cambridge London
66. von Widekind S (2003) The dual theory of choice under risk versus expected utility theory - an analysis with regard to a common generalization. Diplom Thesis, Bielefeld University, Bielefeld
67. Yaari ME (1987) The dual theory of choice under risk. Econometrica 55:95–115

Lecture Notes in Economics and Mathematical Systems

For information about Vols. 1–519
please contact your bookseller or Springer-Verlag

Printing: Krips bv, Meppel, The Netherlands
Binding: Stürtz, Würzburg, Germany